PRAISE FOR *FLIPGRID IN THE INTERACTIVE CLASS*

"Having long been a champion of stude   d, I love
this book! The Merrills have put toget   teacher
maximize this amazing video-response too.   book, you
will find guidelines, resources, etiquette, and lesson plans   rock!"

—Kasey Bell, teacher, author, speaker, blogger at *ShakeUpLearning.com*

"If you are looking to transform your teaching so that it will make a greater impact on student learning, then put this book on your must-read list! The Merrills provide practical and creative applications for using Flipgrid to make any classroom more interACTIVE."

—Julie Smith (@JGTechieTeacher), K–5 edtech consultant,
blogger at *The Techie Teacher*

"When we look at our books, the best ones are the ones with folds and creases inside. Why? Simple, these are the ones we return to over and over again. *Flipgrid in the InterACTIVE Class* is one of those books! With creativity and community, Joe and Kristin have shared within its pages their knowledge, experiences, resources and love of Flipgrid, not only leading educators with the practicalities but, most importantly, settling the 'Why' questions. Get your sticky notes ready—you are going to need them! Thank you, Merrills!"

—Paul Lanny Watkins (@Lanny_Watkins), teacher, MIE Fellow,
Global Learning Mentor

"Together, Joe and Kristin have provided educators everywhere with the pedagogy playbook of the year. Full of practical tips (like the five Fs of Flipgrid) and mic-drop quotes you'll highlight and tweet out, this book has the power to change your practices and positively impact kids forever."

—Becky Keene (@beckykeene), author, *Sail the 7 Cs with Microsoft Education*

"*Flipgrid in the InterACTIVE Class* is the perfect resource for understanding how Flipgrid has become one of education's most pivotal tools. The Merrills detail everything from beginner level status to mic-drop activities, and they infuse pedagogy throughout. The ideas in here are ones that you will want to try in your classroom tomorrow!"

—Mike Tholfsen, principal product manager, Microsoft Education

"Joe and Kristin Merrill have done it again! Their new book is a celebration of learning and page after page is filled with interACTIVE ways to bring student voice to life. Not only are there insights and ideas to help you learn how to use Flipgrid, there are also incredible lessons and activities you can use immediately to transform how students share, celebrate, and showcase their learning. *Flipgrid in the InterACTIVE Class* is a creativity boost that will inspire you and encourage you to think outside the box and find new ways to empower every voice."

—Ann Kozma (@annkozma723), educator innovation lead, Flipgrid

"Kristin and Joe bring experience, passion, and positivity to all that they do—keeping teachers and students at the center of their extraordinary work and practice. In *Flipgrid in the InterACTIVE Class,* they invite educators to join them on their journey to transform teaching and learning as they share ways to innovate with interactive technologies and instructional design. This book is a perfect choice for classrooms seeking ways to prioritize engagement, student voice, digital citizenship, and, of course, fun! *Flipgrid in the InterACTIVE Class* is the ideal ready-to-go resource for today's classroom teacher!"

—Dr. Jennifer Williams (@JenWilliamsEdu), education activist, professor, author

Flipgrid

IN THE
INTERACTIVE
CLASS

ENCOURAGING INCLUSION AND STUDENT VOICE
IN THE ELEMENTARY CLASSROOM

Foreword by Jornea Armant, Flipgrid's Head of Educator Innovation at Microsoft

JOE AND KRISTIN MERRILL

Flipgrid in the InterACTIVE Class
©2021 by Kristin Merrill and Joe Merrill

For information regarding permission, contact the
publisher at info@elevatebooksedu.com.

This book is available at special discounts when purchased in quantity for use as premiums, promotions, fundraising and educational use. For inquiries and details, contact the publisher: info@elevatebooksedu.com.

Published by ElevateBooksEdu

Editing, Cover Design, and Interior Design by My Writers' Connection

Library of Congress Control Number: 2021930944
Paperback ISBN: 978-1-7352046-1-1
Ebook ISBN: 978-1-7352046-2-8

This book is dedicated to all our past, present, and future students.

We hope you harness the power of your words and use them to make great changes.

May your voice be loud and your impact go far.

CONTENTS

FOREWORD

REVERSE POEM

If you can think it, you can Flipgrid it!
The possibilities are limitless,
opening the doors of minds and souls
to learn, share, listen, and grow.

We are in this world,
as educators
for a greater purpose.
Igniting a passion for learning
as we serve our communities.

You are the *magic,*
educators!
Do not be afraid
to be pilots of learning,
who love, grow, and inspire
individual journeys in life.

Fostering connections because
firsthand listening and learning =
what matters in life!

What matters in life =
firsthand listening and learning,
fostering connections.

Because individual journeys in life,
who love,
grow and inspire
to be pilots of learning.

Do not be afraid,
educators,
You, are the *magic*
as we serve our communities,
igniting a passion for learning
for a greater purpose.

As educators,
We are in this world
To learn, share, listen, and grow.
Opening the doors of minds and souls.

The possibilities are limitless.
If you can think it, you can Flipgrid it!

As an educator for over eighteen years, I've always been fascinated with the power we possess in education. With great power, comes great responsibility to do good and be catalysts in our students' learning trajectory, recognizing everyone has a different path. We encourage our students to discover themselves through reflection, grow themselves by learning from others, and support them in being agents of positive change for their communities and the world. This journey begins with curiosity! It is our duty to know *who* is on the journey, why their curiosities exist, and *serve* as curators for students to explore information, challenge ideas, seek out diverse perspectives, question the norm, learn from their process, and ultimately find their magic and purpose in life.

Throughout these years, technology has been a key element in opening more possibilities for educators to broaden the resources students learn with and perspectives students learn from. I've always loved learning about new technologies that could make a difference and transform learning experiences. As a connected educator, who uses social media to learn from other educators, I discovered Flipgrid! It is a simple video tool that allows educators to post a Topic for students to respond to, which creates a social learning environment. Upon my first use in 2016, my mind was filled with so many ideas and opportunities that Flipgrid could provide as a vehicle to meet the needs of *all* learners. The ability for all students to share, learn from each other, and have constant access, all in one organized space that didn't take up storage on my computer was enough for me to immediately fall in love! But the possibilities didn't end there.

Challenges and limitations spark innovation. I was one person, serving as an instructional technology specialist for twelve school districts with hundreds of schools, thousands of teachers across all disciplines, and I wanted to ensure I was able to provide opportunities to learn, connect, and support throughout their professional learning journey. I saw Flipgrid as a means to defy the barriers of time, space, and demand. Working with educators across all disciplines, specialties, and age levels, I also assisted them in leveraging Flipgrid to create meaningful and authentic learning experiences while meeting their students' learning needs. I was so excited about the impact, it was only natural to share the excitement with others. What's great about education is that we have a world of professionals that we can share it with! I started to see, listen, and learn how other educators were using Flipgrid in creative ways, and in that journey, I met the Merrills.

Each day, as I scroll through social media, I am inspired by the joy, energy, and excitement that Joe and Kristin share about what they are doing in their classroom to ignite a passion for learning. In 2017, I joined team Flipgrid as head of educator innovation. In that first year, I knew I wanted to be in their learning environment and experience the magic myself. In February 2018, I traveled to Florida to visit educators on my Savvy Field Trip to see best practices in action. The moment I stepped into Joe's first-grade classroom, I felt sunshine radiating throughout the room, and I knew I was once again in *my happy place*, an interactive classroom!

It was Read Across America Week, and Joe's first graders just finished connecting virtually with another first-grade classroom to share a read aloud. The class seamlessly transitioned into independent and group learning. Some with iPads in hand, others around a kidney table reading, and some were investigating science concepts using multiple types of media. It was a classroom filled with empowered learners! Stepping into Kristin's classroom, I was immediately able to see why they are such a dynamic duo. Her students were creating glyphs based on their love for the stories they were reading. As the students worked, Joe, Kristin and I talked about ideas that could transform those practices. One idea bounced off another idea, and that was the moment I knew *this was something special.*

You see, an interactive class isn't about only students learning. It's really about an educator continuously learning and seeking out opportunities to design learning experiences that empower students to go beyond any limits that are set because learning is limitless. Collaboration with fellow educators opens dialogue to share ideas, resources, and impact, causing a collective efficacy that allows everyone to be confident and supportive when trying something new.

If you're reading this now, welcome to a wonderful community of interACTIVE educators, who love, grow, and inspire their students through learning experiences! Enjoy empowering every voice and remember "If you can think it, you can Flipgrid it!"

JORNEA ARMANT
FLIPGRID'S HEAD OF EDUCATOR INNOVATION AT MICROSOFT

OUR FLIPGRID JOURNEY

JOURNEY *NOUN*

\ˈjərnē/ \

PASSAGE OR PROGRESS FROM ONE STAGE TO ANOTHER.

TheMerrillsEDU !

Teachers love free stuff. That's probably because, all too often, teachers spend their own money on decorations, lessons, and activities for their classrooms, which is why we learn early in our careers how to make the most of donations, gifts, free trials, giveaways, bonus bucks, freebies, and prizes. If something—anything—is free, most teachers are willing to try it.

That's how we found Flipgrid in 2017.

Kristin checked the hashtag of one of our favorite Twitter chats and saw that the chat, which had taken place the previous night, had gone a bit differently than usual. Rather than answer the questions on Twitter, the chat's participants had been asked to answer on a new video platform: Flipgrid. Anyone who participated in the chat received a free account. The goal, of course, was to introduce teachers to this new tool. To Kristin, getting a free account to use the platform sounded great. What an awesome promotion! The problem was that she was a day late.

It *never* hurts to ask for what you want. We learned that piece of advice many years ago from fellow educator Ron Clark and have made it our motto. After all, the worst someone can say is no, but you won't get anything unless you ask. So that is exactly what Kristin did. She tweeted the company asking for a chance to try Flipgrid in her classroom. Much to her surprise, someone responded within that same lunch hour and honored the deal; in fact, the company gave Kristin two trials—one for each of us to use.

The platform's worth spoke for itself; we loved it! But what really resonated with us as we learned how to use Flipgrid was the community behind it. If we had a question, we could tag @Flipgrid in a tweet and receive an answer within a few minutes. If we were having trouble getting something to work, help was just an email away. The team at Flipgrid were (and still are) always listening.

Word spread quickly about Flipgrid, and within a short time educators all over the world had caught the #FlipgridFever. (The #FlipgridFever hashtag caught on so quickly with the platform's excited users that Flipgrid used it to launch its first Twitter chat.) The platform grew exponentially each month, and as it grew so did the family of educators who generously shared ideas and success stories about how this tool was changing learning in the classroom.

We could go into a detailed journey of our involvement with Flipgrid, but there really is no need, because that is not the purpose of this book. Let's just say that the years since that 2017 Twitter chat have been filled with some

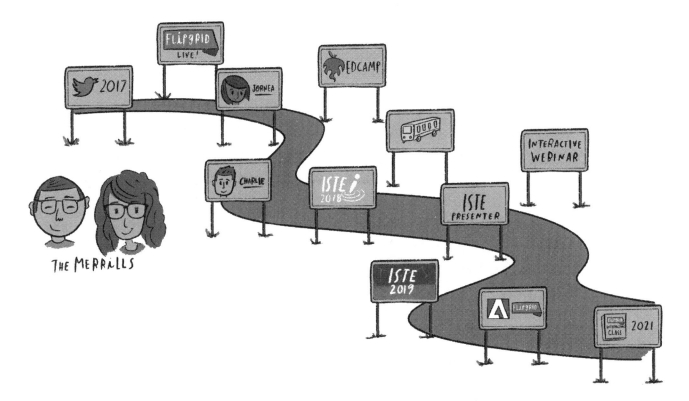

pretty incredible memories. We've had the opportunity to share our Flipgrid experiences and classroom successes with educators across North America. From a traveling training tour to ISTE presentations, we have been hard at work, telling teachers and administrators about the capabilities and possibilities of using Flipgrid in the classroom. And now, with *Flipgrid in the InterACTIVE Class*, we are excited to share our Flipgrid tips and strategies with you.

A FLIPGRID FREE-FOR-ALL

#FlipgridFever is still real and spreading, and that's a good thing! It is our job as educators to use the time students spend in the classroom in ways that create learning moments that lead to lifelong memories. It is these memories, which are formed more by *how* we teach than *what* we teach, that students take with them from our classroom. Flipgrid equips educators to make learning both meaningful and memorable. Through discussion, creation, and collaboration, students create memories that challenge, encourage, and engage them along their journey.

Flipgrid joined forces with Microsoft, and together these companies are working to make Flipgrid accessible to every educator. #FlipgridForAll is the new hashtag and goal, and it's a goal that is attainable because Flipgrid is now free. Free. Yes, you read that correctly. Flipgrid—with its storytelling camera, and its extensive educator community—is free to every teacher on the planet.

FLIPGRID IS NOW FREE. *FREE.* YES, YOU READ THAT
CORRECTLY. FLIPGRID—WITH ITS STORYTELLING CAMERA,
AND ITS EXTENSIVE EDUCATOR COMMUNITY—IS FREE TO
EVERY TEACHER ON THE PLANET.

TAKEAWAYS

If I am walking with two other men, each of them will serve as my teacher. I will pick out the good points of the one and imitate them, and the bad points of the other and correct them in myself.

—Confucius

Throughout our Flipgrid journey, we have learned so much more than how to use this powerful tool. Sure, the features are great, but the family that surrounds Flipgrid is even better. As teachers, we need community and support as we test our creativity by experimenting with new lessons and increase our confidence and willingness to try new things.

Community, creativity, and confidence are traits that we believe you can develop and hone along the way as you experience the support of other educators and the joy of empowering student voice.

COMMUNITY—The Flipgrid community is like none other. From the company's staff members to the educators who use the platform, the global bond formed by those using Flipgrid is unparalleled. Whether you need help, are looking for a new idea, or are seeking validation for a new lesson activity, someone is always waiting to encourage you. This community is fun, uplifting, and always evolving as people work together to make sure that learning is reflective and responsive to the needs of today's students.

Get connected with some of our favorite follows in the Flipgrid community!

CREATIVITY—Flipgrid's platform is built to challenge and encourage creativity. Using stickers, fonts, camera edits, and filters, educators can give students the freedom and flexibility to share their voices in unique and inspiring ways. In addition to giving students a creative platform on which to share their voice, Flipgrid also provides educators a space where they can creatively design interACTIVE and engaging lessons centered around their students and their personalized learning goals. These creative lessons can then be shared on social media to inspire and encourage others in their classrooms.

CONFIDENCE—Fear keeps people from trying new things: fear of failing, fear of being judged, fear of things not turning out as planned. Educators are not immune to these fears, and the reality is that trying new things is never easy. It is also true, however, that a special kind of learning occurs in the process of trying and persevering through something that stretches one's abilities.

If you are looking for some help getting started with Flipgrid, check out these resources!

The Flipgrid team continues to work hard to make the platform easy to use and to provide support for those who need it. In addition, the accessibility tools that are built in give any user a voice and thus confidence to share in whatever their learning environment may look like.

Flipgrid will open a window into your students' thinking and allow them to explore within a safe environment ways to express their thinking and share strategies with authentic audiences. Flipgrid will allow students to learn ways to communicate ideas respectfully and learn how to be thoughtful when speaking with others.

—Heidi Samuelson (@swampfrogfirst)

When this book went to press, more than 100 million educators, in more than 190 countries, had already created accounts with Flipgrid, And those numbers continue to grow! Just as it has transformed our classrooms, Flipgrid is changing what learning looks like around the globe.

We feel fortunate to have had the opportunity to work with the Flipgrid crew and are happy to share our support for the platform with anyone willing to listen. We hope that our love of Flipgrid spills out through the pages of this book in a way that inspires you to use this powerful and empowering platform with your own students. Flipgrid has become a staple in our interACTIVE classrooms, and for that reason, we believe it is our duty to share this platform and our love for it with as many educators as we can.

FLIPGRID REFERENCE GUIDE

TOPIC	Topics are discussion prompts that you create; your students respond to that prompt with a short video.
TITLE	A short, thirty-five-character-maximum title for the Topic
GROUP	Groups allow you to organize Topics under one easy-to-remember join code, so your learners have access to all the Topics you've put into that Group.
PROMPT	A question or stimulus for the Topic. Check out the Discovery Library for ideas!
MEDIA	Add a Topic video, image, gif, or a featured link.
ATTACHMENT	Add up to nine external links to websites such as OneNote, Google Docs, or YouTube that can be included when creating a new Topic.
COMMENTS	Allow students to reply via video to another student
LIKES	Off by default, you can allow students to like other student videos. There is no way to track which specific student likes a video.
VIEW COUNT	Each view is counted as soon as you tap play. There is no way to track which specific student views a video.
STICKY NOTE	Students can take notes using stickies before or during recording. These are not saved after submitting.
FEEDBACK	Educators can provide text, video, or scored feedback. Customize your rubrics for your needs.
STATUS	Active = students can record Frozen = students can only view videos Hidden = students can't access the Topic or any videos
RECORDING TIME	Maximum recording time of student videos: fifteen seconds to ten minutes.
SCHEDULE DATES	Launch Date = schedule when a Topic goes from Hidden to Active at 12:01 a.m. Freeze Date = schedule when a Topic goes from Active to Frozen (view only) at 11:59 p.m.
FLIPGRIDAR	Flipgrid videos can now be viewed in augmented reality with FlipgridAR! Add QR codes to your students' artwork or within books, scan using the Flipgrid app, and watch the video come to life!
MIXTAPES	Mixtapes allow educators to showcase student videos from across any Topic and easily share videos with others! This is a view-only set of videos hand selected by the educator.
ACCESS CONTROLS	Groups and Topics can have their own access controls. Students can join a discussion by accessing a Topic directly or by accessing a Group and selecting from all the Topics within the Group.
VIDEO MODERATION	Off = students will see each classmate's videos. This is default for all new Topics. On = new videos will be hidden and only visible to the teacher.

LAYING AN
INTERACTIVE FOUNDATION

Before we take a deep dive into all the reasons we love Flipgrid and exactly how we use this powerful tool in the classroom, we need to lay the proper pedagogical foundation.

It's going to be no surprise to hear that we believe the foundation begins with an interACTIVE approach to teaching. We will start with creating connections through inviting student voice into the classroom. From there we'll explore what it means to equip and then empower students to use their voice on a larger platform through technology and the combined power of social and global learning.

THE POWER OF STUDENT VOICE

Chapter 1

FOUNDATION *NOUN*
/foun'dāSH(ə)n/
A BASIS ON WHICH SOMETHING STANDS OR IS SUPPORTED

TheMerrillsEDU

For years, the student council and debate team were the only outlets students had to express their voices at school. Although these were (and still are) great extracurricular activities, participation in these groups is limited, as are opportunities for authentic contributions and conversations. In the past ten years, however, the practice of empowering student voice in the classroom and individual learning has grown in popularity. This practice is a distinct alternative to more traditional forms of teaching and learning, in which administrators and educators make decisions with little or no input from the students themselves. Empowering student voice isn't a fad; it's a vital practice for ensuring that learning is meaningful and memorable and done in a way that empowers and uplifts everyone.

The mission at Flipgrid is to empower every learner on the planet to share his or her voice while respecting the diversity of others' voices. It strives to provide a platform that is inclusive, safe, flexible, creative, and simple. Flipgrid is much more than a team composed of international developers and engagement leaders. Flipgrid is the collection of learners and educators who share their unique voices every day in an effort to build a better future. This diverse community of developers, leaders, educators, and learners share an unwavering commitment to student voice that makes Flipgrid stand out from other education applications.

WHAT IS STUDENT VOICE?

Student voice refers to the opinions, values, beliefs, perspectives, and cultural backgrounds students bring to their classrooms or learning environments. When students are empowered to share their voices, they are free to express who they are, what they believe in, and why they believe what they do with their peers, parents, and teachers as well as their entire community.

To be meaningful, student voice must be inclusive, and it requires more than simply listening to our learners or making sure each one has an equal chance to speak in class. Student voice is also about more than giving students a chance to speak up during a parent conference or time to share a portfolio of work. Student voice is more than just asking for an opinion through a survey or questionnaire. Student voice is more than allowing students to play a representative role at a leadership meeting or on a school committee.

Student voice is about listening to learners and then giving their voices power. Listening to the collective voice of students means that we listen and respond to what really matters to them.

STUDENT VOICE IS ABOUT LISTENING TO LEARNERS AND THEN GIVING THEIR VOICES POWER. LISTENING TO THE COLLECTIVE VOICE OF STUDENTS MEANS THAT WE LISTEN AND RESPOND TO WHAT REALLY MATTERS TO THEM.

Check for Student Voice in Your Classroom and School:
- Are students' beliefs and values being respected?
- Are their opinions being heard?
- Are their varying cultural backgrounds being expressed?
- Can students' influence be seen throughout campus?

POWER OF STUDENT VOICE

In a typical, traditional classroom, students may participate in learning projects or take responsibility for different classroom jobs, but in most instances, the teacher determines the students' roles and responsibilities as well as the topics they learn about. Teaching in a way that empowers student voice transforms our classrooms into student-centered environments. The challenge lies in creating a space where students *own and drive their learning.*

We have a lot to learn from our students. We need to share both leadership and power with them. Student voice is not just about giving students the opportunity to communicate ideas or share opinions, but rather it is about empowering them to leverage those ideas and opinions to create change. We need to provide students with opportunities to become leaders in schools. This happens when we trust our students, listen to their voices, and give them power to make change. Then students can take real ownership of their learning, their classes, and their schools by being a part of decisions that are being made. When we increase student voice in schools, we will then succeed in mobilizing students to help initiate and implement educational change. This type of change is where all the power of student voice lies.

> STUDENT VOICE IS NOT JUST ABOUT GIVING STUDENTS THE OPPORTUNITY TO COMMUNICATE IDEAS OR SHARE OPINIONS, BUT RATHER IT IS ABOUT EMPOWERING THEM TO LEVERAGE THOSE IDEAS AND OPINIONS TO CREATE CHANGE.

In addition to learning differently, students these days often think differently than we do. Students have unique perspectives about their classrooms and schools, perspectives that adults don't always share. Our learners, when given the chance, can bring to the surface tough issues that their teachers and administrators may not address—or even be aware of—including structural biases found within the school itself. When students know that their voices matter and they feel supported and empowered, they step up, realizing they can make a difference in others' lives and in their own. Encouraging student voice helps our learners develop skills needed to become involved and productive citizens, such as public speaking, tolerance, and effectively questioning authority. Student voice inspires and empowers those around them to take charge and make change.

STUDENT VOICE INSPIRES AND EMPOWERS THOSE AROUND THEM TO TAKE CHARGE AND MAKE CHANGE.

Finding the balance between too much and too little involvement as we guide our students and help them discover their voices can be a challenge. If we direct too much, we may soften their voices and block our students from becoming true problem solvers and stakeholders. If we direct too little, the voices of our students may become ineffective or diffused. Even as they are empowered to speak up, make choices, and drive changes, students still need adults who are willing to mentor and listen as they work to make meaningful contributions to the teaching and learning taking place inside the classroom.

> When I think of *student voice,* I think of all of the ways that students can share their voices. Student voice means student empowerment. It's about providing students opportunities to share their voices and feeling empowered to do so frequently in the learning process.
>
> —Karie Frauenhoffer (@legitkfrauey)

WHY STUDENT VOICE MATTERS

Think about the lesson that, no matter what you do, how you dress up or transform the room, students just aren't into it or just can't seem to understand. Think back to the motivation of students during that lesson or unit of study. Now think about what might happen to the level of student engagement if you turned that topic of study over to the students and built a lesson of study together. When more directly involved, students inadvertently become more engaged and interested. Their curiosity in turn leads to discovery, taking an otherwise boring and drab lesson and transforming it into something personal and relatable.

To truly teach our students, we must be willing to learn from them. That said, giving up (some) control and allowing students to take on more responsibility can be scary. It requires being open to something not going the way you planned—and maybe even having a lesson take a completely different turn. As we explained in *The InterACTIVE Class,* however, the best learning often happens during those hard and scary moments—when you don't know what's coming next or you're trying something new.

When we take on a mindset that is open to the unfamiliar and choose to empower student voice, we establish a bond between us and our students, a bond that shifts learning from being exclusively cognitive to an experience that meets the needs of learners on an emotional level. We all know how discouraging and frustrating it can be when we feel like our voice isn't being heard. It makes us feel like we aren't valued. That is the last thing we want our students to feel! For students who are struggling to find their place, knowing that their voice is being heard can help them see that they are not alone.

Student voice gives students a sense of belonging. It helps them feel attached and involved—not only in their learning but also in their relationships with their peers and teachers. One of the best ways to influence student achievement is by creating a learning environment in which students feel like they have a stake in their learning. The more choice, control, challenge, and collaboration offered to students, the more their motivation and engagement rises. This sense of belonging will continue to grow as they develop their own sense of identity and increase their ability to think critically.

Beyond meeting students' emotional and relational needs, when we rely on student voice, we increase opportunities for meaningful, personalized learning. Personalized learning cannot happen without student voice. How can we know how to best provide instruction for our students if we don't know how they learn or what they care about? Student voice is essential to making learning personal.

PERSONALIZED LEARNING CANNOT HAPPEN WITHOUT STUDENT VOICE. STUDENT VOICE IS ESSENTIAL TO MAKING LEARNING PERSONAL.

Students who believe they have a voice are also more likely to be academically motivated. Making your classroom student-centered, including promoting student voice and choice, will increase achievement and motivation. Participation improves and behavioral problems decline when students are engaged in challenges they chose to pursue. In short, students' effort and level of persistence are directly related to their motivation and engagement, which is directly tied to student voice.

Beyond the obvious of students speaking, it's the whole package! Student voice is the sharing of understanding, the spark of information, the demonstration of a skill that gives us as educators a window to the incredible mind of our students. When we empower that voice, it builds confidence, it strengthens a community, and it is a catalyst for new ideas to be thought of and shared to challenge and move us forward together.

—Andy Knueven (@MrCoachK15)

HOW TO ENCOURAGE STUDENT VOICE

The traditional, formal methods of including student voice in schools, such as participating in student councils and debate teams, are still worthy of employing. You can even encourage students to take the discussions of these groups a step further by joining or supporting advocacy groups or writing letters to legislators or community leaders. Informal ways of listening to students and getting them involved in the decision-making process include surveys and discussions around current events in which students can share opinions about what is happening both locally and globally.

When preparing instructional materials, topics, and assignments for students, try encouraging student voice by giving students options. Allow them to choose the format in which they will complete and submit assignments. Give them the option of choosing the exact class project to participate in together or allow them to work on a local issue collaboratively.

We can foster student voice in our learning environments in any number of ways, most of which fall into any of four specific categories: facilitating input, representation, self-expression, and exercising voice. These categories serve as guidelines for inviting more student voice into the classroom—starting today.

FACILITATING INPUT

As educators, we need to make sure that we are encouraging our students to share their ideas on a regular basis. A good way to do this is by designating a space in the classroom where students can leave comments, ask questions, and state ideas, share their likes, and offer suggestions for improvements. Another great way to facilitate student input and encourage student voice is by brainstorming with students and creating lists of things they would be interested in learning. Together, we can then find ways to blend our students' interests into the learning environment.

> Students have the opportunity to voice their opinions and perspectives about their learning. Teachers who value student voice base their instructional strategies on student choices and interests.
>
> —Stacy Benton (@sbentonteach)

REPRESENTATION

Seeking out work that represents the perspectives and interests of all learners is important. This is true for texts, Web-based content, speakers, poetry, music, and blogs. The content used in class should reflect the diversity of the student body and of our global society. The best way to create true representation of your students is to seek out work that was created by individuals who reflect the students in your class and community.

SELF-EXPRESSION

Public speaking is not something that comes naturally to most of our learners. It is a skill that needs to be developed. You can empower students to share their voice effectively by teaching them how and why to use "I" statements, eye contact, and body language. Be mindful as you teach these skills that the goal is not to change *how* they speak or how they pronounce their words. Appreciating student dialect and accents is a topic worthy of an entire book on its own. Your goal as an educator is to help students effectively and efficiently communicate their ideas in ways that will increase the level of listening by others around them.

YOUR GOAL AS AN EDUCATOR IS TO HELP STUDENTS EFFECTIVELY AND EFFICIENTLY COMMUNICATE THEIR IDEAS IN WAYS THAT WILL INCREASE THE LEVEL OF LISTENING BY OTHERS AROUND THEM.

Sharing ideas with others publicly is the ultimate goal, but realistically this is not something that every student can do easily or right from the start. Often students are shy, scared, and uncomfortable sharing their ideas. This fear stems from insecurity, and students may need time before they feel empowered enough to share their idea in front of others. We can encourage these quieter, more timid student voices by providing them with a safe place to share their personal thoughts and feelings, removed from the ears of everyone else. Simply start with a moderated Group or Topic, where students can express their ideas and beliefs privately with the teacher and receive the affirmation needed to build confidence and move toward more public speaking.

EXERCISING VOICE

Finally, we need to teach our students to exercise their voices. This can be done through activity-based learning as well as through feedback. Students can exercise their voice by identifying real-world problems that are of interest to them and then working together to form strategies and solutions that will make a difference.

Student voice can also be exercised through the art of discussion. Flipgrid Topics give students the chance to share their thoughts about a specific topic, brainstorm ideas, problem solve, or share personal opinions before discussing with the entire group. If an idea is particularly popular or of interest to students, an educator can spark the discussion into an entirely new standalone Topic for students to use to continue the conversation. Individual student blogs are another simple way to provide a platform for students to exercise their voice and share their ideas through pictures, video, and text.

When I hear the term *student voice,* I think of students being comfortable expressing themselves both academically and emotionally. To me, student voice means that we are cultivating a generation of educated thinkers who are not afraid to speak out about what is going on in the world.

—Sachelle Dorencamp (@SachelleD)

In addition to exercising voice through learning activities, we should also give students the opportunity to share their voice through feedback. *Feedback* generally is used in reference to the teacher giving thoughts, opinions, or comments to students based on work they have turned in. But what about providing students a chance to give the teacher feedback? Student feedback doesn't have to be limited to a lesson or learning unit. Allow students to give feedback on the classroom itself and their learning experiences as a whole. This feedback can then be used to make effective changes in the learning environment and in future lessons and activities. Giving students a chance to share their perspectives about the learning environment and their experiences will provide valuable insight on how to improve instruction going forward.

In our interACTIVE classroom and in classrooms worldwide, Flipgrid empowers student voice in numerous ways. In Part 2 of this book, we'll share a variety of lessons and strategies for integrating Flipgrid to encourage students to share their voice, demonstrate their critical thinking skills, and show their level of understanding. One of the things we love most about Flipgrid is that it engages students in meaningful, active learning. Every time we hear educators describe Flipgrid, they use verbs—action words—to express how this powerful platform enables students to demonstrate their learning, share their unique perspective, and make sure their voices are heard.

PIVOTING YOUR PEDAGOGY

Chapter 2

PEDAGOGY *NOUN*
/ˈpedəˌgäjē/
THE METHOD AND PRACTICE OF TEACHING, ESPECIALLY AS AN
ACADEMIC SUBJECT OR THEORETICAL CONCEPT

TheMerrillsEDU

*P**edagogy.* This strange word is used frequently in the world of education, but what is it? What does it really mean? Is it a science or maybe a theory? Is it based on actions or the ideas of people who came before us? Does it exist without feedback or assessment, and can your personal values fit within it? Is it just a fancy synonym for the art of teaching?

Maybe.

For centuries, this one word has been used to describe the study of teaching and how content is presented and delivered to a learner. Pedagogy originally referred to the *theory* behind why educators did things a certain way. Today, however, the word is used more commonly in reference to the *practice* of that particular theory. Teachers study the objectives, processes, and desired outcomes and then use those theories to craft hands-on lessons. In short, educators use the term *pedagogy* today to sum up the art and act of teaching.

Teachers hold vastly different pedagogical views. The countless variety of school structures, teaching models and curriculum, and learning materials used around the world offer evidence that no two teachers think exactly alike. Each teacher's pedagogy is the product of education, unique experiences, and personal beliefs.

Belief drives action, and therefore pedagogy. But what happens when beliefs are not founded on facts? The outcome in that case is faulty action and faulty pedagogy, neither of which is good for students.

BELIEF DRIVES ACTION, AND THEREFORE PEDAGOGY.

Let us explain.

Beliefs commonly form based on the behaviors we see modeled and fads that pop up on social media. Unfortunately, many behaviors and fads have little, if any, grounding in evidence. Because these behaviors and trends are what we see, experience, and subsequently implement, we cling to them year in and year out, believing they are good. These beliefs, even though they lack evidence, become part of the pedagogy that guides our teaching and influences our strategies, activities, and assignments. When that happens, we get stuck in a rut created by convenience, tradition, and popularity, rather than basing our actions on sound pedagogy, which requires far more intention.

Throughout the discussion of pedagogy in this chapter, we hope you will ask yourself these questions:

- *What is my personal teaching philosophy?*
- *What do I consider to be indicators of great teaching?*
- *What has influenced my teaching practices?*

Good pedagogy is vital to effective teaching. As educators, we must be intentional about recognizing why we do what we do and analyzing the beliefs that drive our actions and teaching.

RELATIONSHIPS AND PRACTICES THAT PROMOTE GOOD LEARNING

What you do as a teacher makes a difference to your students' growth and success. In other words, high student performance comes from quality teaching. And you won't be surprised to learn that we believe the most important factor for student achievement is *interACTIVE* teaching. Regardless of the theories and ideals that make up your pedagogy, interaction (aka *relationship*) should be at the heart of it; good pedagogy and interACTIVE teaching and learning are all about the relationship between a teacher and a student—a relationship that prioritizes the learner's needs.

When you develop a relationship with your learners and prioritize their needs, you will be concerned with the things that concern them. Rather than remaining in a rut of static teaching and unfounded beliefs or ineffective practices, you will seek out ways to empower students by helping them understand not only what they are learning but *why* they are learning it. You will equip your students to face the challenges they encounter and make sure they know how to ask for help and whom to seek out when they need assistance.

Good pedagogy cannot exist without putting learners first. When your approach to teaching aims to meet your learners' needs, your pedagogy will change over time. Pedagogy is often spoken of as though it were fixed and repetitive, but we believe that it should evolve with experience and advances in technology. Additionally, personal pedagogy evolves (or should evolve) as the world changes. Health concerns, population diversity, global warming, shifts in our economy and employment, technological trends, and diversity and equity issues are a few of the realities that constantly shape and reshape the way educators think. Being intentionally aware of the impact that these societal and cultural influences have on your students can improve your teaching and, thus, your students' learning.

GOOD PEDAGOGY CANNOT EXIST WITHOUT PUTTING LEARNERS FIRST. WHEN YOUR APPROACH TO TEACHING AIMS TO MEET YOUR LEARNERS' NEEDS, YOUR PEDAGOGY WILL CHANGE OVER TIME.

INTERACTIVE PEDAGOGICAL PRACTICES

As we mentioned earlier, everyone's personal pedagogy is unique, and we believe it is important to be mindful of the elements that constitute our personal pedagogical practices. When we are mindful, we become intentional, insightful, and systematic. Mindfulness allows us to consider not only the wellbeing of our students but also the type of learning that takes place in our classroom.

In addition to acknowledging and celebrating the differences that each teacher brings to their work, we also recognize that a few specific pedagogical elements should be adopted by every educator. Those elements include student voice, metacognition, building on background knowledge, assessment, inclusivity and diversity, and using a variety of teaching models.

STUDENT VOICE

We discussed the power of student voice at length in the previous chapter, and we want to mention it again. Student voice is essential to good teaching. Without it, we make assumptions and generalizations about how our students feel. Without an outlet to share their voices and express their opinions, student perspectives remain invisible.

WITHOUT AN OUTLET TO SHARE THEIR VOICES AND EXPRESS THEIR OPINIONS, STUDENT PERSPECTIVES REMAIN INVISIBLE.

In contrast, when students have the opportunity to share their voice in a learner-centered environment, both the teacher's practice and the students' learning improve. Allowing space for student voice improves academics and increases engagement and motivation. Think about it: When students are given the opportunity to produce something with their teacher—rather than simply *for* their teacher—they are inevitably more motivated to assist in the future, thus maximizing their productivity in the classroom.

When they know their voices are heard in the classroom, students develop a sense of agency, and hopefully they cultivate a desire to speak out and make their voice heard in their communities and far beyond.

As with any practice, you also need to be ready to accommodate the students who do not wish to participate or find it difficult to speak their minds. These students can contribute in different ways but may not feel comfortable speaking up. That's when we have to implement strategies to ensure that even quiet students have a voice.

Using Flipgrid's platform is the easiest and most effective way to start when it comes to adding student voice in the classroom. It provides educators with a free space that they customize to fit the specific learning needs of their students. Flipgrid also provides students with a safe (and often private) space to share their ideas, concerns, and knowledge of the world around them.

> Providing students with choice and encouraging them to share what they are learning with an authentic audience should be a foundational practice in all classrooms. Empowering students to share what they are learning helps them become more proficient learners.
>
> —Heidi Samuelson (@swampfrogfirst)

METACOGNITION

The push toward higher-order thinking is nothing new to the education world; in fact, you may already use various types of questions and questioning strategies in your classroom. From Bloom's Taxonomy to Webb's Depth of Knowledge, likely you have sat through multiple training sessions focused on the types of questions that can be used with students. And for good reason! Questioning is a great way to challenge your students' thinking, and their answers provide you with a clearer and more direct way to give feedback.

Two types of questions are used in most classrooms today: procedural and learning based. Unfortunately, most of the questions asked are procedural.

Are you finished yet?

Did you put your name on your paper?

Do you have any questions?

Procedural questions constitute the bulk of interaction with students in many, if not most, classrooms. These are not necessarily bad questions, and they may even be necessary. But they are not the types of questions that lead to higher-order thinking, otherwise known as *metacognition.*

Metacognition, defined simply, is "thinking about your thinking." Learning-based questions require metacognition. These types of questions are open-ended and not related to basic recall. They require analysis, not repetition.

When planning your lessons, considering the learning-based questions you want to ask is important, because they are unlikely to just come up during class discussions. Write out a few questions, remember that less is more—fewer questions actually require more thinking. Your goal is to gradually lead your students through basic understanding to a point where they begin contemplating the more complex tasks.

In addition to developing metacognition through questioning, it comes into play when using Flipgrid. Unfortunately, so many teachers use technology in the classroom in ways that merely substitute a screen for a sheet of paper. Filling in the blank, matching, and dragging words or images into a specific category are substitution tactics. Even if these activities appear to engage students, they require little to no metacognition.

In contrast, when students press record in Flipgrid, they are instantly augmenting any type of paper-based assignment you may have previously used in class. The ability to share their voice, record their thinking, reflect on their own ideas, and then share with others is a complete game changer that demands a high level of mental processing.

BUILDING ON BACKGROUND KNOWLEDGE

A foundational brick in the interACTIVE pedagogy is the process of building lessons based on students' background knowledge. For students to conceptualize material, they need to be able to take the knowledge they have already acquired and use it to build on the new learning being presented. As teachers, our job is to help students connect the old information to the new through understanding. As students develop the ability to build on old learning, they gain a sense of pride, confidence, and achievement.

QUESTIONS TO ASK WHEN TRYING TO BUILD ON BACKGROUND KNOWLEDGE

- Does this activity begin by connecting student knowledge with home, community, or school?
- Are the activities being designed with local meaning for students?
- How am I assisting my students with making connections?
- How am I creating opportunities for family members to get involved in the lesson or unit?

ASSESSMENT

Assessment is a familiar term when referencing pedagogy, but it is a foundational element in the interactive pedagogy. When you read the word assessment, a test may be the first example that comes to mind. The words test and assessment are two different things, however. A test is a product given to students to measure a specific goal or objective. It examines one's knowledge of a topic or formula. A test is easy to grade, and the results do not have to be interpreted. Spelling or grammar tests, math facts, and sight words are a few familiar tests with clear-cut, right-or-wrong answers.

Assessments differ from a test in that they can be used both *during* and *after* instruction. An assessment documents the learning that has taken place by evaluating student knowledge, attitudes, skills, and beliefs. The responses that students give during an assessment can be used to alter instruction if needed. In a nutshell, a test is a *product*; an assessment is a *procedure*.

A TEST IS A *PRODUCT*; AN ASSESSMENT IS A *PROCEDURE.*

In an interACTIVE classroom, the goal is to prioritize students and ensure that the teaching meets their learning needs. Assessments enable us to be responsive to those needs. They give us the opportunity to interpret the effectiveness of our teaching and make decisions regarding what happens next, and they alert us as to whether we need to alter our plans. When used appropriately, assessments can be powerful and insightful and can enhance our teaching.

Our goal as educators is for students to leave our class with mastery of content, and as with all worthwhile goals, mastery may take multiple tries. When we test our students, give a grade, and then move on, we may be failing to ensure that mastery.

OUTCOMES OF TESTS	OUTCOMES OF ASSESSMENTS
• Train students to conform to performance strategies • Cause students to compare themselves with other students • Goal-oriented motivation (teacher-set) • Low long-term success	• Learning is invoked • Learning is compared with content, not students • Students learn to self-regulate their own learning • Teacher reflection encouraged • High long-term success

Of the two most popular types of assessments used in classrooms today—summative and formative—we believe formative assessments are critical in the interACTIVE classroom. Formative assessments range from formal procedures to informal checks used during the learning process. Teachers can use the responses to modify teaching and learning activities, with the goal of improving student achievement. Formative assessments are intended to measure where students are in the learning process by applying a diagnostic tool, usually in the form of questions.

Flipgrid is the perfect platform for formative assessment. Teachers can pose a question to students in Flipgrid, giving students the freedom of choosing how they create and share their answers. They can record an answer, write one out, animate it, or hide their face and just share their voice. However students choose to respond, the outcome for the teacher—a clear insight into their learners' knowledge or understanding—is the same because each student answers the same question. It's voice, choice, metacognition, and assessment all in one simple platform.

INCLUSIVITY AND DIVERSITY

For a long time there has been confusion between equality and equity. Instead of focusing on equality and treating all students fairly, equity in the classroom can be defined as giving students what they need. In an interACTIVE classroom, we as educators need to help our students turn away from fairness, and rather teach them the history and psychology of racism, encouraging critical conversations around these issues with them based on their age. In an effort to be equitable, we as educators are obligated to create, gather, and curate curricula that allow us to build lessons in which all are represented and accounted for. This may mean we have to unpack personal biases, teach beyond our provided texts, and model for students the type of thinking and activism needed in today's classroom. When we truly listen to students and respect in the classroom is mutual between students and us, a productive classroom can be formed.

Flipgrid's platform is built on inclusivity and diversity and on ensuring the unique voices of *all* students are heard. Through the various partners in Flipgrid's Discovery Library—Langston League, ADL Education, and Made by Dyslexia to name a few—Flipgrid creates safe learning environments where all students feel represented and included. In addition to the Discovery Library, Flipgrid also supports the mission of diversity through Grid Pals by enabling teachers and classes to connect with people all over the world. Through this simple platform, you can instantly connect with more than 30,000 educators worldwide!

Check out some of our favorite lessons from the Discovery Library focused on inclusivity and diversity.

> I believe it is essential that every student has the opportunity to express themselves, contributing his or her ideas and creating products as opposed to always consuming content! Therefore, it is essential that teachers ensure students have equitable opportunities to create and express themselves.
>
> —Christine McKee (@CMcKee27)

USING A VARIETY OF TEACHING MODELS

In the interACTIVE Class, an integral part of the pedagogy you develop needs to be centered on *how* you deliver instruction to your students. The way you plan, deploy, and assess each lesson needs to be tailored based on the task at hand. The teaching models you use in class need to be varied and diverse. They need to include a mixture of whole group instruction, inquiry-based projects, independent work, and technology-infused instruction. It is also important to find the balance between activities that are collective, cooperative, and competitive.

We are so passionate about using a variety of teaching methods that we wrote an entire book about it: *The InterACTIVE Class*. In this book, we have an entire section of lessons devoted to Flipgrid because its platform encourages creativity, collaboration, and out-of-the-box thinking for the teacher and student. Flipgrid provides amazing variety, from tangible and gamified lessons that use QR codes and FlipgridAR to private and collective thought processing features such as moderation and Mixtapes.

THE LEARNER IMPACT OF GOOD PEDAGOGY

Like any other idea, structure, or principal that we implement in our classrooms, the goal is for it to have a positive impact on our learners. Technology, tools, and teaching fads change daily, but strategies and pedagogy remain constant. The things that make a good learning environment do not change; rather, they build on each other year after year, creating a solid instructional foundation. Our outcome as educators is ultimately a product of our foundation. The things we build our classroom on will directly influence and affect the type of learning that takes place there, the kinds of learners we develop, and the ways our students think about the world around them. The three following learner outcomes benefit the classroom experience and the student for years to come.

OUR OUTCOME AS EDUCATORS IS ULTIMATELY A PRODUCT OF OUR FOUNDATION.

COMFORTABLE SHARING

The ability to communicate is probably one of the most essential skills needed in the workplace today. You may be one of the smartest and brightest employees, but if you are unable to communicate and work with others, the length of your employment may not correlate with your IQ. Cultivating conversations gives students an opportunity to not only speak but also listen to the voices of others while reflecting on their own views. It helps open their minds to new ideas while sharing and speaking with classmates.

CONNECTED CONCEPT

A solid pedagogy helps to create an environment in which students feel connected and valued. As you equip students to connect past, current, and future lessons, you will see strides in their academic achievement as well as in their ability to connect learning to their personal lives, an outcome that multiples the impact of an interACTIVE class.

Flipgrid makes it easy for students to record at home, in class, or anywhere where they have access to a mobile device. This gives them the opportunity to share and continue their learning far past the four walls of the classroom and to connect their learning in school to their life at home.

CLEAR UNDERSTANDING

When students have a clear understanding of the curriculum and the expectations of a class, their engagement and participation increase. As they learn what works for them as learners—what their unique learning style is— they will be able to participate in ways that are personal and tailored to their needs and interests. As students learn how to share their voice and demonstrate their knowledge using Flipgrid, they gain a clearer understanding not only of the information but also of themselves. It's when they are able to articulate their thinking that they really have a firm grasp of it.

When we are aware of our pedagogy—what goes into it and what needs to be a part of our teaching—choosing applications and platforms to integrate into the classroom is easy! It is through this kind of self-reflection that we and thousands of other educators have come to appreciate the benefits of Flipgrid. In this single platform, students have an outlet to share their voice and ideas, build and reflect on learning, and demonstrate their critical thinking. We have more to say about this platform, of course, but these capabilities alone would be enough to make Flipgrid a necessary tool for any modern, interAC-TIVE classroom.

SOCIAL LEARNING IN THE MODERN CLASSROOM

Chapter 3

ENGAGEMENT *NOUN*
/inˈājmənt,enˈājmənt/
ANY ACTION TAKEN BY A SOCIAL MEDIA USER ON YOUR PAGE,
SUCH AS LIKES, REACTIONS, SHARES, OR COMMENTS

TheMerrillsEDU

Social media is part of our world. Even if you don't use social media yourself, chances are, it affects you simply because so many your coworkers, your students, and their parents use it. Now, we're not telling you that you have to be on social media, and you certainly don't have to use every platform or app out there to understand its usefulness. You should, however, be aware of the services and apps your students are using. These apps are how this generation of learners connect and communicate. It is here where they are influenced, where they get their ideas and beliefs—for better or for worse—and knowing about this part of their world can help you better relate to and interact with them.

During the past ten years, technology has become an integral part of many classrooms. Educators today can choose from a plethora of devices, programs, applications, and information to use and share in their classrooms. The upside of this plethora of available technology is that it gives schools, districts, and universities cost-effective ways to provide a quality education to a broad, even global, audience. It also helps educators maintain flexibility in both delivery and content while increasing accessibility for all types of learners. Technology allows us to create and provide authentic, relevant, and global learning experiences while infusing collaboration into lessons that would otherwise feel stagnant and segregated. If there is a downside, it is that the sheer number of options requires teachers to constantly balance the *what* with the *how*, and most importantly, the *why* behind the technology and applications they choose to bring into the classroom—including social media.

For our purposes, when we refer to social media, we are talking about websites and applications that enable users to create and share content or participate in social networking. At the heart of all social media—whether it's Facebook, Instagram, Twitter, or even TikTok— is the ability for users to generate connections. And if one thing is certain, it is that social media is here to stay, which means we must treat it as a resource we can use in our classrooms to leverage learning rather than as a distraction. Social media is simply one of many tools that you can use to make your classroom more engaging, relevant, and culturally diverse. To ignore it or forbid its use in our classrooms is to do our students a disservice.

We get it. We understand the concern that to allow tech devices and social media use in the classroom is to open the door to distractions. Students will chat, snap, and tweet while we teach, right? Maybe. And if they are bored, definitely. But remember that long before smartphones existed, students found ways to occupy themselves when they were bored in school. The antidote to boredom and cure for distraction is engagement. If we want students to engage, we need to make them participants in the learning process.

IF WE WANT STUDENTS TO ENGAGE, WE NEED TO MAKE THEM PARTICIPANTS IN THE LEARNING PROCESS.

Our students are often the best authorities on what is useful and of interest. Find out what tools they're using and take time to check out those tools for yourself. You might find them helpful, or you might not. But learning about what your students are using and recommending opens you up to new tools. More importantly, it shows your students that you respect them and care about what is important to them.

Rather than dismissing social networking applications, start asking how they could be useful to your students. Are there ways that social media could benefit your students by helping to fill in the gaps in learning if used in a safe and appropriate way? Could you use social media applications to build stronger relationships within the classroom? In our own classrooms, we've found the answers to both of those questions to be *yes*. We've also discovered that when we use technology to help students feel connected and included, they become interactive participants in class.

> My classroom is built on the idea of social learning. Involving and accepting the opinions of every student is what drives my instruction.
>
> —Yaritza Villalba (@inc_yv)

Interaction and connection are two powerful benefits of using Flipgrid in the classroom. It is a social learning app that is packed with features students recognize, know, and love to use. Flipgrid gives our digital natives a comfortable space to share their voice, using a tool that feels similar to the popular clip-creating, video-sharing platforms they already enjoy.

BENEFITS OF USING SOCIAL MEDIA IN THE CLASSROOM

Educators can use social media to develop creativity in their students by encouraging them to explore content material in a variety of ways; in fact, there are many benefits to integrating social media into modern learning environments. Let's take a look at just a few. Social media can be . . .

A PLATFORM FOR DEMONSTRATING LEARNING

One of the biggest benefits of using social media is that it gives students the ability to demonstrate their learning. As students produce their own media, they discover a sense of pride that comes with creating and sharing their work. Sharing can be done through blogs, podcasts, videos on YouTube, and most notably, Flipgrid.

A TOOL FOR STUDENTS TO COMMUNICATE AND COLLABORATE WITH ONE ANOTHER AND THE TEACHER

Humans are very social beings. We are in constant need of community. Social media makes connecting easier and faster than ever. Through the use of social media, we can develop learning environments in which rich learning experiences rely on connection and collaboration, and this connection will give our students the opportunity to communicate quickly and easily. Gone are the days when a student had to wait until the next day to ask the teacher a question on their homework or clarify directions with a friend over the phone. They can communicate with anyone at any point in time if connected virtually.

A WAY TO CONNECT WITH LEARNERS AROUND THE WORLD

Social media gives students the ability to communicate with other students around the globe. Students can connect via chat, voice-over-internet calls, or video conferences, using a device that fits in their pocket or backpack. Through social media, students can open up the window to the classroom, carry on discussion outside of the traditional school day, and keep in touch with people in places where, ten years ago, direct communication was impossible.

A PLATFORM FOR CONNECTING WITH EXPERTS, AUTHORS, AND LEADERS

When students have questions or want to dig deeper on a topic, social media provides an avenue for communicating with experts virtually. Teachers can set up video conferences, using tools such as Flipgrid, so that students can meet and talk with book authors, scientists, or people who lived through historical events such as the Holocaust. Connecting through social media is less expensive (*free*) and simpler than trying to organize travel, and the students feel a deeper connection with the content when they can interact with a person who experienced or produced it. These networks of learning can develop and grow over time, creating quite a community of learners.

A TOOL TO INCREASE STUDENT ENGAGEMENT

Using social media in the classroom increases student involvement. Students are more willing to connect when they can use technology to research information, share ideas, and produce final products. As student involvement increases, so does their investment, which will lead to a sense of ownership from students. Designing lessons that ask students to use social media as they work also helps to build their confidence, generate enthusiasm, and foster a sense of play in the learning process.

A MEANS OF INCREASING PARENT INVOLVEMENT

Social media can help parents stay in touch with what is going on in the classroom. Whether it is through a class Facebook page or a school Twitter account, social media gives parents a place to get updates on school-related activities, projects, and events in real time. Social media can give parents a window into the classroom so that they can observe and share in their children's academic progress and personal growth at school.

A WAY TO IMPROVE TECHNOLOGY FLUENCY

It seems as though a new app comes out every day, and although these programs, including social media platforms, may appear to have different purposes, the foundational structure of most apps is quite similar. Icons for adding video, editing clips, inserting text, and commenting are similar across platforms. The similarity means that as students spend time using social media they are also becoming more fluent and comfortable with necessary technology skills. In other words, using social media as a tool in the classroom is a natural way to develop technology fluency among learners.

> It's funny because these education and social media often seem at odds to some, but I think the two go hand in hand with giving us the capacity to reach out, connect, learn from one another, and lean on each other.
>
> —Erin Holland (@erinjurisich)

GUIDELINES FOR IMPLEMENTING SOCIAL LEARNING

The decision about which social media platforms to use in the classroom should not be based on what applications are popular but rather on which tools are most relevant and effective in the learning space. Educators must balance the technology they choose for the classroom, especially social-based applications, with their preexisting pedagogy. The goal is to leverage technology and integrate it into the practices and theories that are already proven and valued. It's this combination of technology and pedagogy that creates meaningful learning outcomes. No tech device or social media platform on its own can influence learning outcomes, improve metacognition, or increase cognitive development. Social media without learning design is simply social.

SOCIAL MEDIA WITHOUT LEARNING DESIGN IS SIMPLY SOCIAL.

So how do we create meaningful learning opportunities using social media tools? As with almost everything else, the decisions we make need to be based on the specific learners in our current classrooms, their ages, and their unique interests. Next let's review some guidelines for what to focus on when incorporating social media into the classroom.

DESIGN LEARNING ACTIVITIES THAT ARE RELEVANT AND APPLICABLE TO CURRENT AND FUTURE WORK ENVIRONMENTS.

Today's students never experienced a world without the internet. Think about that. Our students today cannot remember when the first cell phone was invented or tell you where they were when they first learned how to use the internet. They have grown up watching YouTube, streaming on Twitch, and creating content to document their lives.

The prevalent access to information via smartphones and tablets has conditioned children to rely on technology to find answers to simple questions and solve basic problems. Knowing how to find information is an important skill to develop, but we also must ensure that our students learn how to think, reason, and problem solve without relying on technology to tell them the answers. YouTube, for example, is a great source for how-to videos. But there may not always be a video available. We need to make sure we are putting our learners in situations where they are forced to solve problems on their own.

As we work to incorporate social learning into our classrooms, our methods need to create learners who approach issues and situations in such a way that they acclimate to and solve problems, rather than simply coming to the table relying on personal, preexisting knowledge. Being able to communicate with teachers, with students, and with the outside world are all vital skills for the world of work and college. The goal is to produce students who can go out into the world and solve problems, not just look to other people or technology for solutions.

THE GOAL IS TO PRODUCE STUDENTS WHO CAN GO OUT INTO THE WORLD AND SOLVE PROBLEMS, NOT JUST LOOK TO OTHER PEOPLE OR TECHNOLOGY FOR SOLUTIONS.

PROVIDE GUIDANCE AND SUPPORT.

In addition to choosing the appropriate forms of and times for social media, we need to make sure that we provide students with clear guidance and support throughout these types of lessons. Digital citizenship skills are too often overlooked when introducing social learning lessons to our students, and it is our job as educators to not only lead them to the resources, but also model how to appropriately use them. Like any tool, social media can be used wisely or poorly. Students who are given opportunities to engage with this tool in positive ways, such as publishing their ideas, promoting social justice, and discussing important topics civilly, will learn to make appropriate choices. Whether it is something as simple as leaving a comment on a Flipgrid video or something more advanced, such as creating a YouTube channel, we need to empower our students by guiding them in the proper ways to use social media. Here are a few questions for you to consider when you bring social media into your classroom:

- What is appropriate to post?
- Whom should you interact with?
- Are we matching the type of social media to the learning outcome we are trying to achieve?
- Should you "friend" or follow your students or make your posts accessible to them?
- What makes social media valuable, and why are we using it in class?
- Are there certain types of posts to avoid?
- How can you control who has access to what you post?
- How can social media be overstimulating, and what can we do to stay focused?

INCORPORATE HOLISTICALLY. ALIGN ALL TECHNOLOGY, INCLUDING SOCIAL MEDIA, WITH COURSE GOALS, OBJECTIVES, AND ACTIVITIES.

Be intentional about designing a student-centered learning environment in which learners have flexibility in decision-making while still working toward specific learning objectives. By aligning the use of social media and incorporating social learning activities directly with your class goals and objectives, social learning seamlessly becomes part of the learning environment, not something added on top of it; for example, if you normally have students debate the points of a historical event, you can integrate the use of social media by allowing them to conduct their discussions on a platform such as Twitter. Students could create a hashtag to track the conversation and even structure the discussion points ahead of time, arranging them into a chat-style format.

PROTECT STUDENT PRIVACY.

Before using technology or any social learning platform with your students, familiarize yourself with it. Take the time to understand its privacy settings and terms of use. Almost all platforms have settings that allow you to control who sees what and in what specific ways. Keep in mind that anything sent via email, text, or through other electronic platforms has a potential to be copied and pasted elsewhere.

Regardless of whether your account is public or private, you need to be careful about posting photos of students if parents have not signed the school's media release documents. Avoid using first and last names of students, the name of your school or district, and any other personal information when using social media platforms, to help keep students safe.

RESOURCES FOR INCORPORATING SOCIAL MEDIA

Many teachers can see the value of using a student's social world to generate interest and to foster engagement, but more times than not they are unsure of where to start. Sadly, social media gets limited to passive consumption or as a substitution for another form of media (e.g., textbooks or worksheets). Seeing a teacher using a YouTube video to present information to students, for example, is commonplace. Students watch videos, gathering information for research and reporting purpose. Unfortunately, that's as far as the use of social learning goes in the lesson.

When seeking opportunities to integrate social learning into your classroom, consider the following formats and uses and choose the option that work best for your classroom setting:

Research	In addition to being a resource for researching current events, social platforms provide opportunities to teach students about sources, biases, and information authenticity.
Interaction	Open the doors and break down the walls of your classroom by using social platforms to interact with classrooms around the world. Learn about new cultures while giving students a chance to connect with students like them from around the world. Social media platforms also allow family members to interact and be part of the learning happening in the classroom. Whether your students are connecting with people in town or far away, integrating social learning empowers them to share their work, their learning, and their voice.
Collaboration	Social learning is a perfect way for students to practice interacting and working with others toward a common goal. They can combine skills and share ideas to solve problems—in the classroom, in the local community, and even with learners and leaders around the world.
Reflection	Social platforms can serve as a space for students to reflect on current events through the actions, thoughts, and postings of others. In today's world, major news is often first reported by the people experiencing it firsthand. Trending hashtags and geo tags allow you to stay current with events happening in real time. Social platforms also provide students with a space to share their thoughts and feelings through stories, posts, and videos that can be housed on blogs, websites, and popular social media apps.

GETTING STARTED WITH SOCIAL LEARNING

We hope that by now we've convinced you of the value of social learning and that you are ready to incorporate social media into your classroom. So where do you start?

IDEAS FOR ELEMENTARY GRADES

Using a social media platform may not be an option if you are working with young students. Some platforms have age requirements, and some school districts prohibit social media use for elementary or primary grades. You can still create social learning experiences using other lesson formats, such as texting, or applications such as Google Slides or Microsoft's PowerPoint.

> As an educator, I use social media to gather ideas, share what I'm doing, and create a network of like-minded individuals. I think you can create these same scenarios in the classroom for students. If it's something students use constantly (social media), adapt it to what you're teaching.
>
> —Jennifer Mahin (@jennasaurustech)

TEXTING—One of our favorite ways to mimic social media platforms is through texting. Students love to text, so why not adapt this communication method for the classroom? Have them take on the perspective of a famous icon in history, retelling an event from their point of view. Or maybe they analyze an event from a story or share how a character changed throughout the text. Texting Story and iFake Messages are applications that make it easy to integrate the feeling of texting in the classroom in a safe and structured way. These "texts" can also be uploaded to a Flipgrid topic in the form of video and images, which students can then explain further by simply pressing record!

TEXTING STORY

IFAKE MESSAGES

DIGITAL SLIDES TEMPLATES—Creating look-alike templates that mimic popular social media platforms is another option to use with young learners. Try creating slides that look like an Instagram feed, in which students create a profile, add an image, and post a caption. If you're not sure how to create these templates, have no fear!

Check out some of our favorite resources and sites for free templates here.

| SLIDES MANIA | CYNTHIA NIXON | RYAN O'DONNELL | MATT MILLER |

IDEAS FOR MIDDLE AND HIGH SCHOOL GRADES

If you teach older children, especially those thirteen years and older, we encourage you to test out a few social media platforms by incorporating their use into your normal lessons. Now, as with any new strategy or tool, if implementing it doesn't work, take time to reflect on what happened, pivot, and then try again. If the social media tool proves to be a distraction or an inefficient way for students to demonstrate their learning, then it may not be the right fit for that particular group of learners. That is okay.

 Tip: Remember that any Google Slides template can be converted into a PowerPoint presentation. Simply open the slide deck and hit File > Download > PowerPoint (.pptx).

Once you are comfortable using social media platforms yourself and you have the okay to do so from your administration to use them in your classroom, get started with one or more of the ideas below. Many of these ideas could be adapted for multiple platforms, including Facebook, Twitter, Instagram, Snap Chat, or Flipgrid, giving you the freedom to choose the platform you feel best fits your students and the learning environment.

- Create a class blog for discussions.
- Document class adventures and field trips.
- Incorporate podcasting at either the class or student level.
- Create a class-specific Pinterest board.
- Use Instagram for photo essays.
- Feature a student of the week.
- Create class polls, using specific hashtags.

- Ask students to write about the significance of a posted photo—perhaps a map, person, or document.
- Share classroom news with parents and faculty.
- Showcase student work.
- Create a class message board.
- Have students create their own class show or school announcements.
- Use a group to stream live lectures and host discussions.
- Assign blog posts as essays.

Students are going to communicate, collaborate, create, and publish online with or without the help of educators. The digital environment we have available to us is capable of providing students with some of the greatest opportunities they've ever had, and they are most likely missing out. It is going untaught. Whether it is out of fear, misunderstanding, or perceived lack of value, we need to challenge ourselves and our own thinking, and begin to embrace this form of learning while finding ways to embed it into our own classrooms. With such a wide range of platforms available, we can find ways to use social media in our lessons that promotes critical and creative thinking from students about the world around them and their place in it.

DEVELOPING DIGITAL LEARNERS

Chapter 4

EVOLVE *VERB*

/ ē'välv/

DEVELOP GRADUALLY, ESPECIALLY FROM A SIMPLE TO A MORE COMPLEX FORM

TheMerrillsEDU

As technology continues to improve and its everyday use increases, so does our dependence on the internet for day-to-day tasks such as purchasing products, accessing bank accounts, and staying in touch with those close to us. We have access to more information through various platforms and more exposure to the world around us than ever before. Much of education and communication today happens online, and it's our responsibility as educators to extend the walls of our classrooms to include these new digital spaces. With this exposure and access comes a responsibility—for us and for our learners. Our goal is to teach students how to navigate this digital world responsibly and to help them develop healthy relationships with the world around them in the process. Simply stated, we want our learners to develop good digital citizenship.

Digital citizenship can be explained simply as the responsible use of technology—whether using a computer, scrolling through the internet, or working on a digital device. Good digital citizenship helps us build and maintain connections both in and out of the classroom. Teaching digital citizenship equips our students with skills, knowledge, and resources to succeed as lifelong learners and helps them engage in a digital environment with confidence. This confidence will then help students develop into leaders who are equipped to make a meaningful impact on the world around them. Simply said, a student's digital capability is a direct extension of their digital competency.

SIMPLY SAID, A STUDENT'S DIGITAL CAPABILITY IS A DIRECT EXTENSION OF THEIR DIGITAL COMPETENCY.

WHY TEACH DIGITAL CITIZENSHIP?

Online safety is one of the most essential and influential elements that come out of teaching digital citizenship. Lessons surrounding safety include avoiding inappropriate websites, notifying a trusted adult of information or encounters that are not appropriate, and refraining from posting personal information online. These are all lessons we can teach students to help keep them safe when working and learning online.

When we teach digital citizenship to our students, the benefits extend far beyond the classroom environment. By working to develop these specific skills in our students, we are helping to create a safe and secure space not only for them but also for everyone with whom they interact. Students who are taught online safety also develop a sense of digital confidence and are less likely to fall victim to threats that await online. Online safety is vital in keeping students safe in their digital space so they can grow up to be empowered digital citizens.

> It is important to teach digital citizenship as intentionally as English Language Arts or Math. We need to build students' skills in being a responsible and productive digital citizen. Our students need to know how to safely navigate online spaces to drive their education, vocation, and perspective.
>
> —Nyree Clark (@MsNyreeClark)

Teaching digital citizenship skills can also help bridge digital equity gaps between students. The disparity between those who have access to current digital tools and those who do not is often referred to as the *digital divide*.

Some of this disparity is the result of location and living in a place that does not have the infrastructure built in to support modern-day access. Most people who live without internet, however, do so because they cannot afford it.

Not all students have the same access to technology at home or are exposed to the same digital experiences, which means that we educators must include resources and lessons about digital citizenship in the classroom. We also must provide them with the technology to use while doing so. We can then develop digital citizenship as a core element, and the resources and lessons used in school can help those students catch up with their classmates.

Finally, teaching good digital citizenship can help stop and prevent cyberbullying. Cyberbullying is an increasing cause for concern for both teachers and students. Establish guidelines and start with lessons that cover responsible online communication, repeating and reinforcing them often. Make sure to set clear boundaries regarding appropriate online interactions. You can even create a list of digital citizenship rules with your students. These Dos and Don'ts can be posted in the classroom and reviewed often. Encourage students to be open and to report any behavior that makes them uncomfortable. For students who find it harder to come forward, Flipgrid has integrated the use of AI to help protect students when using the platform. All comments and user-added text, videos, thumbnails, and video transcripts are scanned for bullying or offensive content, with educator notifications and automatic moderation built in. This feature helps students navigate the digital space on Flipgrid with kindness and empathy while helping the educator monitor and manage all the discussions.

WHAT SKILLS DO WE NEED TO TEACH?

When working with students online, digital citizenship is our umbrella. It encompasses the norms of appropriate and responsible behavior we expect students to have when using technology. Many different skills fall under this umbrella, including digital literacy, digital etiquette, digital communication, digital rights and responsibilities, and digital access. By teaching digital citizenship skills in our classrooms, we can give students the right tools to use when engaging with the digital world. These tools will enable them to engage in ways that promote healthy online communities. In most elementary classrooms—especially those using Flipgrid—the concepts of digital literacy and digital etiquette are two of the more prevalent skills from the digital citizenship umbrella that we tend to focus on.

DIGITAL LITERACY

The American Library Association (ALA) defines digital literacy as "the ability to use information and communication technologies to find, evaluate, create, and communicate information, requiring both cognitive and technical skills." If our goal is to have our students creating, collaborating, and sharing digital content within the classroom, we need to then make sure they know how to do so responsibly. In today's digital world, nearly every career requires digital communication in some form or fashion. It is essential, then, that we equip students with the skills to effectively and responsibly find, evaluate, communicate, and share online content. We believe that to help prepare them for this future, the benefits of teaching your students digital literacy skills begin in the classroom.

Finding information in today's learning environment is not a problem for students. With so many resources just a click away, students have access to information like never before. Fake news, click bait, spam, and advertising are all commonplace on the web. Students are faced with a new challenge: they have to sift through it all, understand it, and then be able to identify which elements are applicable for the task at hand. What good are 150,000 search results if a student doesn't know how to differentiate between the useful information and the junk? It is our job to teach them how to figure out what is real and valuable—and what isn't.

Students also need to learn about embedded resources, such as hyperlinks, audio clips, graphs, or charts, which require them to make choices. Teaching digital literacy empowers students with the skills and understanding necessary to not only use the internet and technology to their benefit, but also to use it in the most effective and efficient ways. We want our learners to be able to quickly find information and to use the ever-expanding list of sites in meaningful and powerful ways.

For students to develop digital literacy, we as educators must carve out time to teach the specific skills necessary for success. This can include teaching students how to conduct a proper Web search, as well as which sites are reputable to use as reference materials, among other useful lessons, which will differ depending on the age of your learners. The minutes in the day are already precious enough, so often we must find creative ways to integrate this type of instruction. Obviously, it fits best in a weekly technology class or time, but that also may be difficult because of guidelines regarding what is to be covered each week. Teachers are the masters of finding time when there is none to be found, and we can creatively weave digital citizenship skills throughout the teaching of other content; for example, when launching a unit of research, add in a whole-group mini lesson on finding credible sources and how to identify inauthentic websites. If students are demonstrating knowledge through multimedia presentations, spend a class period discussing basic copyright and the legal use of images and other content.

DIGITAL ETIQUETTE

Another tool we can equip our students with when engaging in and with the digital world is etiquette. We've all experienced a lack of digital etiquette—for example, when someone is having a phone conversation on speaker mode in the middle of a restaurant; or when people forget the basic courtesy of turning off their phones before entering a church or memorial service (There's always that one person, right?!).

CHECK OUT SOME RESOURCES HERE!

The concept of digital etiquette is vast and could fill the pages of an entire book on its own. If you are interested in diving in more deeply to the various components and principles that make up digital etiquette, check out the resources curated in the QR codes provided.

Because our focus is on integrating Flipgrid into the classroom, we are going to focus on and highlight digital etiquette as it pertains to filming video responses.

THE ART AND ETIQUETTE OF VIDEO RECORDING

Public speaking is a skill that has been taught (and dreaded) in classrooms since the days of the one-room schoolhouse, where students had to stand up in front of the class to recite their memorized readings and handwritten essays. The invention of the smartphone and tablet camera have reduced some of that fear, replacing it with a sense of confidence in digital natives. Students often feel secure in front of a camera. In this solitary, protected space, they can record their thoughts uninterrupted by the outside world. Even if they fully intend to share those thoughts publicly, being able to record (and re-record if necessary) instills a wonderful sense of bravery.

Today, even the youngest students know how to record a video on a digital device. Our job is to help them learn to do it well. Video is powerful, and when used correctly it can give any voice power and purpose—that is, if the viewer can hear the message clearly and follow what the speaker is trying to communicate. Unfortunately, the portability of the commonplace camera means students can record and share at a moment's notice, which often means that aspects such as focus, audience, and clarity are forgotten.

When teaching students how to use Flipgrid, model the Dos and Don'ts of video recording. Let them see what a shaky video looks like or how it feels to view a message while looking up someone's nose. (Funny, but you know there's always that one child.)

VIDEO IS POWERFUL, AND WHEN USED CORRECTLY IT CAN GIVE ANY VOICE POWER AND PURPOSE—THAT IS, IF THE VIEWER CAN HEAR THE MESSAGE CLEARLY AND FOLLOW WHAT THE SPEAKER IS TRYING TO COMMUNICATE.

Enlist your learners' help in compiling checklists of things to do and to avoid when recording. Model how to record a video well, then compare the result with the poorly recorded video. Have students look at the differences. Which message gave off more confidence? Which message was presented better? Which message would you be more likely to listen to?

THE FIVE FS OF FLIPGRID VIDEOS

Help your students get off to a strong with video recording and responding with the fives Fs of Flipgrid videos:

- **FOCUS**—Before recording, make a plan for your message. Take time to organize your thoughts in a way that clearly and concisely communicates your message.
- **FACE**—Be prepared for what people are going to see when viewing your video. Regardless of whether your face or something else will be on the screen, make sure you take time to think about what others will see.
- **FRIENDLY**—Above all, you need to respect the unique voices of others. Everyone has something valid to share, and we need to be open to listening to what others have to say.
- **FEEDBACK**—In addition to sharing your ideas, make sure to take the time to listen to the ideas of others. Leave kind, meaningful responses when you reply.
- **FUN**—Get creative and have fun! Use Flipgrid to demonstrate your learning and share your voice in ways that represent who you are as a learner and a person!

GET STARTED NOW WITH THIS FREE POSTER TO HANG IN YOUR LEARNING SPACE FOR STUDENTS!

FLIPGRID PRESENTER COACH

In addition to focusing on the Five Fs for Flipgrid recording, take advantage of one amazing integration: PowerPoint Presenter Coach. Now, within Flipgrid, students also have the benefit of using Presenter Coach. Leave it to Flipgrid to realize the amount of work it takes to plan lessons, prep them on Flipgrid, and monitor and instruct further through them. After noticing that the actual skills for presenting weren't being covered in the classroom, the company developed Flipgrid's Presenter Coach to help save educators time and frustration.

As students begin recording, the Presenter Coach will listen to their speaking as they share their ideas. If a student begins repeating words such as *if*, *um*, *like*, or *uh* too often, it will prompt them to "try not to use so many filler words." When a student speaks very quickly because of excitement or nervousness, Presenter Coach will prompt them to "try speaking a bit slower."

Once students are finished recording, they will see a timeline above their video, with pinned spots indicating all the areas they could have improved. Students can hover over these pins to see the exact recommendations. There will also be a report card for students to have during this review time, which will give a summary review of feedback on things such as sensitive phrases, filler words, facial expressions, and pace. If students wish, they can then go into the trimmer view on that video and trim before the error so they can rerecord and replace that segment. Students can add to their video and keep recording until they have a perfect, awesome, totally great video ready to submit!

Presenter Coach allows students to reflect and grow on their terms, with meaningful feedback on their presentation skills, giving educators the time to continue fostering student growth in the learning environment. Because some video recordings are intended to be spontaneous without the need to be final-presentation perfect, Flipgrid Presenter Coach can be toggled on and off per Topic discussion by the teacher.

CREATING SPACES FOR RECORDING

When using Flipgrid, it is important to provide students with appropriate recording spaces. Some learners are comfortable sharing their ideas with others, and for these students simply sitting at their desks or along a counter works well. Other students may prefer a more private place to record that is quiet. This doesn't mean you need to go out and create a class set of recording booths, invest in a bunch of new technology, or refurnish your classroom to use Flipgrid. Students can record in many different locations, using the learning spaces and tools you already have in your classroom.

UNDER DESKS—Sometimes, sitting under a desk or a table can give students a private space to record. And let's face it; getting to sit under the desk is fun for students and allows them to get up out of their seat for a few minutes.

CUBBY OR BOOKSHELF—Giving students the ability to spread out helps cut down on the noise when recording. Simply using a cubby in an organizer or a shelf on a bookcase helps direct sound towards the microphone and makes for a more clear and direct message.

CORNER OF A ROOM—Many students prefer to record in places where others can't see them, and a corner works great for this. They can simply place their device in the corner and be free from distraction while recording, while also creating a more sound-conducive space.

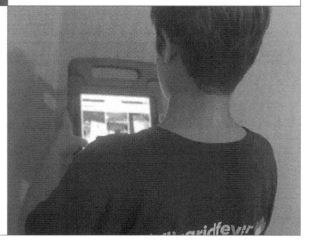

CLIP-ON MICROPHONE—There are always those students whose voice never seems to be at an audible level, and when they record it gets even quieter. Clip-on microphones are an inexpensive way to amplify the volume of students' voices while recording. They also hold up well to the normal wear and tear of any classroom.

WINDOW LEDGE—If you have a hallway or classroom with a window view, try giving students to option to record outside of the classroom. You could create hall passes to help students manage the number of those out at one time. Window ledges also allow you as the teacher to keep your eyes on the students while they work.

TENT—Having a Flipgrid pod is an ideal place for students to record. You can use an inexpensive wardrobe storage from Target or IKEA to create quiet space for students.

 CHECK OUT THIS AWESOME POD IDEA!

RESOURCES FOR TEACHING DIGITAL CITIZENSHIP

Whenever we want to implement a new approach to teaching, we curate a list of resources and tools. Taking the time to research, learn, and try out new programs or tech tools before sharing them with students makes for easier, less-frustrating integration. We've curated the list of resources that follow to help you create your digital citizenship curriculum. Try creating a new Wakelet collection as you explore these resources on digital citizenship, or take a look at the one we have started for you!

CHECK OUT THESE RESOURCES ON DIGITAL CITIZENSHIP FOR KIDS!

WHAT IS WAKELET?

Wakelet is a great resource for any teacher looking to save, organize, and share content from across the Web all in one place. Bookmarking content from across the Web—articles, videos, blogs, tweets and so much more—in just two easy clicks. Then, take those bookmarks and organize and curate them into collections. You can add other images, text, and even Flipgrid videos into your arranged content. Sharing these collections is also very easy and can be done through a single link. Collaborate with others on group collections to facilitate sharing ideas, inspiration, and knowledge. Wakelet has both an app and browser extensions, making it accessible to teachers anytime, anywhere. Learn more by heading to their website below!

THE DIGITAL CITIZENSHIP INSTITUTE AND DIGCITKIDS

DIGCITINSTITUTE.COM/DIGCITKIDS

Bridging the gap between local and global, the Digital Citizen Institute is all about making human connections online. Because its leaders view digital citizenship as an action, and something that students should be taking part in every single day, they created DigCitKids. This online space serves to encourage students to share their voice with the world by solving real problems and creating solutions. The institute's goal is to empower kids with the belief that each person's online actions can travel around the world to inspire others.

COMMON SENSE MEDIA

COMMONSENSE.ORG/EDUCATION/DIGITAL-CITIZENSHIP

Common Sense is the nation's leading nonprofit organization dedicated to providing trustworthy information and education regarding media options. With the mission of helping kids and families thrive, this independent, research-based organization also works to help educators navigate the digital world with their students. Common Sense Education supports K–12 schools with everything educators need to empower the next generation of digital citizens. Its innovative, award-winning Digital Citizenship Curriculum will help you equip your learners with lifelong habits and skills for online use.

BE INTERNET AWESOME FROM GOOGLE

BEINTERNETAWESOME.WITHGOOGLE.COM/EN_US

To make the most of the internet, kids need to be prepared to make smart decisions. Be Internet Awesome teaches kids the fundamentals of digital citizenship and safety so they can explore the online world with confidence. Download their Internet Awesome curriculum, check out pledge posters, and have kids play their way through learning with the site's unique *Interland* game.

MICROSOFT DIGITAL LITERACY CURRICULUM

MICROSOFT.COM/EN-US/DIGITALLITERACY

Digital skills can play a powerful role in helping people connect, learn, and engage with their community—all of which contribute to a more promising future. Through this course you will gain the digital skills necessary to engage in a digital economy and improve overall understanding. This course is used worldwide by individuals, nonprofits, schools, and governments. Microsoft Digital Literacy is for anyone with basic reading skills who wants to learn the fundamentals of using digital technologies.

READING RECOMMENDATIONS

Picture books are a great way to communicate an idea when teaching littles. Through short, summarized messages, kids can learn complicated and serious concepts. We use picture books in our classrooms daily, so we thought we would include some of our favorite picture books when it comes to the topics of digital citizenship, safe technology use, and digital safety practices.

- *Good Night Selfie*
- *Nerdy Birdy Tweets*
- *The Technology Tail*
- *But It's Just a Game*
- *If You Give a Mouse an iPhone*
- *Bully*
- *Troll Stinks*
- *But I Read It on the Internet*
- *The Fabulous Friend Machine*
- *Chicken Clicking*
- *When Charlie McButton Lost Power*

HEAD OVER TO THE BLOG AND CHECK OUT A POST HIGHLIGHTING ALL OF THESE TITLES!

Knowing where to start when it comes to teaching digital citizenship can be a daunting feeling, but in all reality, whatever we do—no matter how small— we are setting the initial blocks in the digital foundation of our students, building toward a goal of safe and responsible digital understanding. We can work today and in the future to embed these important lessons authentically within our content, ensuring that students gradually take ownership of their digital lives and their actions while working and learning online. Keeping our focus geared toward what students should do, rather than what they shouldn't, as educators we can teach this important topic throughout the year, giving our students the skills they will need to succeed as digital learners, leaders, and citizens of the future.

ENABLING GLOBAL LEARNERS

Chapter 5

GLOBAL *ADJECTIVE*
/ˈglōbəl/
RELATING TO OR EMBRACING THE WHOLE OF SOMETHING;
RELATING TO THE WHOLE WORLD

Global learning refers to the cultivation of multiple, diverse perspectives. The intended outcome of global learning is that students appreciate their world (both near and far) and grow up to become proactive citizens. For that to happen, students need to understand how their own beliefs and perspectives shape their environment. More importantly, they need to realize that their beliefs may be very different from others' beliefs—and that differing perspectives are valid. This realization is the starting point for building global learners. And it only happens when our lessons explore and examine past and current political, economic, social, and technological developments to fully develop an interACTIVE understanding of the world around them.

GOALS FOR GLOBAL LEARNERS

1. Students will investigate the world around them beyond their immediate living and learning environment.
2. Students will learn to recognize, understand, and appreciate perspectives of other people.

3. Students will be able to effectively communicate ideas with diverse audiences.

4. Students will be able to translate their ideas into progressive action.

> We can build global learners by making connections with other students outside of our classroom. Connection builds compassion, knowledge, and empathy for others. Students will be able to develop multiple perspectives when they are able to see life through more than one lens.
>
> —Nyree Clark (@MsNyreeClark)

HOW TO CREATE INTERACTIVE GLOBAL LESSONS

As with any type of interACTIVE learning, there is no one right way to reach a goal. Every teacher's toolbox is filled with different resources, tools, and strategies. Regardless of the specific ways you choose to integrate global learning into your classroom, we believe there are three main things all educators should do and consider when working toward creating a global learning environment.

BE INFORMED

Before embarking on a journey to create meaningful, global lessons, it is important to start at home within your classroom. Take time to get to know your students beyond their names, what their favorite subject is, or how many siblings they have. Before you can create interACTIVE lessons that connect and inspire students, you need to know their backgrounds, their struggles, and their passions. Learning with, from, and about your students helps create a safe environment that encourages inquiry and honesty. Weaving their traits, stories, and interests into your lessons will lead students to feel connected, represented, and empowered.

LEARNING WITH, FROM, AND ABOUT YOUR STUDENTS HELPS CREATE A SAFE ENVIRONMENT THAT ENCOURAGES INQUIRY AND HONESTY.

As an educator, it is also important to do your research regarding the global issues and organizations you wish to incorporate into your lessons. We are the first to admit that we are not experts in anything, and often refer to the saying

"Jack of all trades, master of none." We, as many of you, still have a lot to learn when it comes to global issues and worldwide connections, and we are not afraid to admit it. But with that admission comes the acknowledgment that we have a responsibility to do homework before throwing issues and projects in front of students. We need to make sure we are culturally sensitive to what we are putting in front of our students and that we are not being insensitive when discussing global issues.

BE INTENTIONAL

It takes time and repetition to make something routine. Whether it takes twenty-one days, four weeks, or three months, breaking out of a mold and trying something new takes persistence and perseverance. As educators, we need to have a make-it-happen attitude when it comes to creating lessons.

Try starting small with something local that is easy for students to connect to. You can then apply the concepts they learn from local issues to global issues. This progression from local to global will help students better follow, connect to, and understand complex cultural problems.

The following tips may help you as an educator when being intentional with your global lessons and content:

1. Start with a brief overview of the topic before jumping directly into the details.
2. Draw connections between local issues and the larger, global concepts.
3. Present problems that encourage a creative problem-solving approach.

BE INVOLVED

Involvement is simply the act of being a part of something. As educators, we are *(without effort)* involved in the planning and implementation of our daily lessons. Take that involvement and extend it beyond the four walls of the classroom. Gain support for your issue or cause by including students' families and fellow colleagues in your lessons. Create opportunities for those close to students to participate, collaborate, and learn alongside your students. This can be done as easily as teaming up with a global organization to raise money for something as simple as buying farm animals for families in need or helping to build a well that will bring clean water to a town in need. Students and families can learn and work together both in and out of the classroom to achieve the goal set by the students. In addition to getting those around you involved, make sure you show your students your excitement and eagerness to get started. This positive energy is contagious, and it infuses your already interACTIVE lessons with even more energy and engagement.

BENEFITS OF GLOBAL LEARNING

Just like the applications and programs we stock in our education toolkit, global competency is a tool for students to add to their own toolboxes. Developing global awareness makes our students more productive and progressive in their thinking and beliefs and, hopefully, in their future actions.

Now more than ever, our economy is truly global, with millions of jobs in global marketing, sales, and advertising, to name only a few. Employers today are desperate to hire people with cross-cultural skills. They need employees who can thrive in diverse teams and work with clients from all over the world. By providing students with opportunities in the classroom to understand the broader world and the diversity of people, cultures, and perspectives in it, we are also giving them a competitive edge in the marketplace. Global learning allows students to develop skills necessary to become a global citizen; providing students with a global education is the best way to prepare them for their global future.

> Providing students with authentic opportunities to problem solve and think critically about social and world issues introduce students to ideas and perspectives beyond their local community. It also prepares them for the types of tasks they will encounter in the work force.
>
> —Erin Holland (@erinjurisich)

In addition to preparing students for their future role in the workforce, global learning also offers many positive and personal benefits for them in the present-day classroom. When learning with a global audience, students get the opportunity to learn content through authentic tasks and real-world experiences. This type of learning environment fosters student engagement, which in turn leads to higher attendance and achievement. For example, if you are teaching a high school Spanish class, are students more likely to engage with a set of flashcards or would they rather connect with other students living in South America, using Flipgrid? Would they prefer to practice conjugating their verbs and using their vocabulary by filling out a worksheet or by debating current events pulled straight from the headlines?

QUALITIES OF A GLOBAL LEARNER

Global learners . . .

- understand issues from multiple perspectives.
- gain an appreciation and sensitivity for other cultures and a tolerance for religious, political, and cultural diversity.
- are able to articulate ideas in a respectful and meaningful manner.
- apply what they've learned as they function in the global world.
- develop appropriate modes of dialogue and an ability to articulate their ideas clearly.
- strengthen their critical thinking and problem-solving skills.
- become more ethically responsible when making decisions.
- apply more divergent thinking when faced with a problem.
- develop skills over time that make them more technologically literate.

Encouraging an environment of global learning also fosters social–emotional learning within the classroom. Global learning helps students develop *self-awareness* of their own identity, culture, beliefs. Students can then work on figuring out how these personal beliefs connect with the wider world. Skills such as empathy, perspective-taking, respecting others, and appreciating diversity develop over time, along with relationship-building skills, through effective communication and collaboration. These all combine and transfer into something we refer to as social awareness. Learning from and with the world not only benefits students' academic development but contributes to their social–emotional development as well.

> **LEARNING FROM AND WITH THE WORLD NOT ONLY BENEFITS STUDENTS' ACADEMIC DEVELOPMENT BUT CONTRIBUTES TO THEIR SOCIAL–EMOTIONAL DEVELOPMENT AS WELL.**

RESOURCES AND TOOLS TO USE FOR GLOBAL LEARNING

There are many ways to get started as you work toward creating an interACTIVE global classroom. Every year the group of students you have will be different, thus organically pushing you toward new perspectives, experiences, and inquiries, all of which you can use to connect to the current global issues. Let those obvious connections be your starting point. From there, consider your goal. Is it to create global connections, foster global collaboration, or spark student activism? All of the above? With your goal in mind, craft lessons that expose students to global issues while integrating your required standards and content into your daily lessons. Here are a few ideas to get you started.

1. **Investigate the world.** Give students a chance to learn what life is like in places other than where they live. Allow them to ask questions about why things are the way they are and encourage them to analyze and reflect on whether they agree with the ideals, conditions, policies, or subject matter being studied.

2. **Recognize perspectives.** Help students understand how their beliefs create and affect their environment. Challenge students to dive into their own beliefs and to learn about others' perspectives.
3. **Take action.** Students learn by doing! Consider asking your learners to tackle a specific global issue or goal head on. Have them learn about an issue and its causes, and then develop a plan and take steps toward positive change.
4. **Bridge barriers.** Foster communication and connection with learners in classrooms around your community and beyond. When students connect, communicate, and collaborate with peers on the other sides of the globe, they gain a new appreciation for differences and similarities among cultures.

Once you have the focus of your global integrations set, think about what types of content you want to infuse into your interACTIVE activities and units. Some of our favorites include problem-based learning activities, debates, researching using international resources, and inviting guest speakers to come in and share their own experiences. In addition to the way you structure your lessons, the following resources include many different perspectives and activities, giving you a variety of opportunities to infuse global learning in your interACTIVE classroom.

#GRIDPALS (BY FLIPGRID)

WHAT IS IT? A network of Flipgrid users designed to help Flipgrid-using classrooms collaborate and learn together (created by Bonnie McClelland)

KEY FEATURES: The convenient search feature allows the user to filter and find other classes based on grade level, subject, and location.

HOW TO GET STARTED: To access #GridPals, log in to your Flipgrid Educator Dashboard and click on #GridPals at the top. On the next screen, toggle on *Email Invites* to allow fellow GridPals to contact you at your connected email address (please know, your email is never shared until you reply).

CHECK OUT BONNIE'S EBOOK HERE BEFORE GETTING STARTED!

EMPATICO

WHAT IS IT? Empatico is a free tool that connects classrooms around the world. It empowers teachers and students to explore the world through experiences that spark curiosity, kindness, and empathy.

KEY FEATURES: Empatico's free platform empowers teachers and students to explore the world through experiences of others, fostering meaningful connections with other students around the world. Students get the chance to learn about others through scheduled video meets, live interactions, and targeted lessons.

HOW TO GET STARTED: Sign up on the Empatico website, then find a partner class to collaborate with!

TAKE ACTION GLOBAL (TAG)

WHAT IS IT? Take Action Global (TAG) was created to inspire change by providing opportunities for students around the world to give involved in social causes through education. Take Action Global works to help students learn ways they can take action within their own lives to make a better world tomorrow for everyone.

KEY FEATURES: Teachers everywhere are invited to join in for collaborations with thousands of classrooms for social good global projects aligned to the United Nations' Global Goals. Take Action's innovative pedagogy helps connect educators globally to support social good and sustainability through teaching and learning.

HOW TO GET STARTED: Follow TakeActionEDU on social media to stay up-to-date on what is happening next!

#TEACHSDGS (TEACHSDGS.ORG)

WHAT IS IT? #TeachSDG's mission is to help reach their goal of actively supporting and enhancing the work of the United Nations' efforts within K–12 classrooms. Through the Sustainable Development Goals (SDGs), #TeachSDG works to connect dedicated global educators within education while pointing them to lessons, global projects, and other accessible resources aligned to the SDGs.

KEY FEATURES: Connect and collaborate with a broad network of educators, and have your classroom join another to work toward accomplishing the SDGs—all for free. Educators can access curated lists of global videos and use updated resources shared by the UN Global Goals community.

HOW TO GET STARTED: Head over to the teachSDGs.org website and sign up for your desired outcome.

PART TWO

FLIPGRID 101

You've laid a strong foundation. You understand the power of student voice and have taught your students what it means to be a good digital citizen. Now it's time to equip them—and yourself—with a tool that will help them express and share their voice, demonstrate their learning, and make connections in the classroom and around the world. That tool, of course, is Flipgrid.

If this tool is new to you, consider Part 2 your personal guide. This section will give you the information and courage you need to integrate its use in your interACTIVE classroom.

FOUNDATIONAL FEATURES IN FLIPGRID

Chapter 6

TOOL *NOUN*
/tool/
A DEVICE OR IMPLEMENT, ESPECIALLY ONE HELD IN THE HAND, USED
TO CARRY OUT A PARTICULAR FUNCTION

TheMerrillsEDU

Every tool has a purpose and a specific function. When you use the right tool for the job—be it building a house, fixing a car, teaching, or learning—the task becomes easier. As educators our **job is to *equip* students with knowledge, skills, and tools needed to succeed in school and in life.** The tools we use to accomplish this momentous task will vary from paper and pencil to the latest tech device; as we explained in our book *The Inter-ACTIVE Class*, not all tools and valuable teaching practices have to be digital or based in technology. Human relationships, empathy, community, and equity are all things we should strive to infuse our classrooms, regardless of our teaching preferences.

AS EDUCATORS OUR JOB IS TO *EQUIP* STUDENTS WITH
KNOWLEDGE, SKILLS, AND TOOLS NEEDED TO SUCCEED
IN SCHOOL AND IN LIFE.

Similar to a toolbox heavy with hammers, screwdrivers, and wrench sets—or the kitchen drawer filled with cooking gadgets—we all need an education toolkit stocked with ideas, strategies, devices, and applications that we can pull from to make lessons and learning interACTIVE. And the good news is you get to stock your education toolkit with whatever tools best fit your needs. You may prefer to keep a lot of tools on hand so you always have access to exactly the right one. Or maybe you dislike clutter and find that having too many tools in one place makes finding the right one difficult.

Learning how to use a new tool can be time consuming and frustrating. The more versatile and user-friendly a tool is, the more valuable it becomes to the user. This is why, regardless of how full or organized your toolbox is, we recommend that your toolkit include the Swiss Army knife of educational technology: Flipgrid.

THE MORE VERSATILE AND USER-FRIENDLY A TOOL IS, THE MORE VALUABLE IT BECOMES TO THE USER.

Flipgrid can be used in so many different ways and settings! Regardless of the subject, the age of your learners, or their (or your) comfort level with technology, Flipgrid is versatile enough to be used by everyone. This is why, when people ask us what our all-time favorite edtech tool is for the interactive classroom, Flipgrid is the answer. We recommend it for new and veteran teachers alike, for those who are just beginning the journey toward integrating technology in their classrooms, and for educators who consider themselves uber-techy. Here are a few things to consider when selecting any new tool—and a few of the reasons we recommend Flipgrid:

EASE—How long will it take for someone new to learn the platform?

Creating a new Flipgrid account takes only a few minutes, and from there you can easily navigate through Flipgrid, using the tabs on the educator dashboard. Starting a conversation is as simple as logging in, creating a Topic, and sharing out. The streamlined platform gives users an engaging way to express their creativity and learn with and from their peers.

For your students, Flipgrid makes sharing their voice easy. Students don't need individual accounts to record and share. Topics can be shared easily through a unique URL on any platform, a QR code, or a join code. Whether you are team IOS or Windows, iPhone or Android, Google or Microsoft—the beauty of Flipgrid is that it works with all operating systems. It is inclusive not only for learners of different styles but also for educators of different teaching preferences.

VARIETY—Is there more than one way you can use it in the classroom?

Flipgrid is built on the idea of accessibility and flexibility, with the real goal being to amplify student voice. This means that how you choose to use the platform in your classroom is up to you. You can have students creating videos within Flipgrid, appsmash and bring videos in from other applications, link projects and other documents of learning directly within the platform, connect with other classrooms around the world, dive into augmented reality (AR), curate, and so much more!

VALUE—How will using this benefit my students and classroom?

Through links, QR codes, Flipgrid AR, and much more, Flipgrid screams authentic learning. The team at Flipgrid is very passionate about making learning authentic and doing things that give students the ability to share their learning with others both in and out of the classroom.

THE KEY COMPONENTS OF FLIPGRID

The foundational features of Flipgrid can be divided into five main components: the creative storytelling camera, a simple and engaging platform, a powerful educator dashboard, accessibility, and an enriching collection of ready-to-use activities. These main elements work together to make Flipgrid an incredible platform that provides a modern social learning experience. Let's explore the features of each.

A CREATIVE STORYTELLING CAMERA

The Flipgrid Camera is the heart of Flipgrid. It's what you and your learners use to express creativity and tell your stories. As of summer 2020, 2.6 billion videos had been shared on Flipgrid—that's 80 videos per *second!*

CAMERA FEATURES		HOW TO USE THE FEATURE
Filters	Filters give students a fun way to express themselves, and a safe way to share their voice. From colorful gradients to privacy filters such as Block mode, Flipgrid covers the needs of all students.	• Gamify responses by having students guess the speaker or item behind the filter. • Provide a safe space for shy or reluctant students to participate because they can hide their faces or blur out their image from viewers.
Frames	Add some fancy flair to your work with custom frames, such as neon, news, or jungle—courtesy of Microsoft Education!	• Turn students into news reporters with the ability to simulate live news reporting with custom Flipgrid frames. • Frames also can be used in combination with other features to create Flipgrid "scenes" related to the topic being discussed and shared .
Emojis	Emojis add creative flair to videos. You can find these stickers right within the Flipgrid camera!	• Describing characters using emojis is a great way for learners of all ages to communicate ideas. • Emojis can also be used as math manipulatives while students write and explain their thinking. • Emojis can easily be moved around your video while recording, which makes "illustrating" ideas even more interACTIVE!
Text	Fun fonts give students the chance to express themselves in colorful and creative ways. Users can change the font and alter the color, stroke, and background of the text.	• Create titles, headings, and thought or speech bubbles within videos. • Use fun fonts to label the parts of something, or identify objects through a video. • Create comic-style videos, using fonts combined with photo stickers and emojis. • Use fonts to create captions or titles for stop-motion style responses, allowing students to omit audio or voice-over explanations. • Create labels or diagrams of still photos or student-made drawings, using fonts.

Drawing	The ability to ink onto the video is a feature that works both before and during recording.	• The drawing tools give those recording the ability to annotate text live! • Try using the drawing tool to create Flipgrid Book Snaps, in which students annotate and respond to the same text. • The drawing tool is an easy way for primary students to draw over and identify parts of a video or recorded scene. (Head to Part 3 and check out the Living and Nonliving lesson!)
Boards	Boards are backgrounds that can be used while recording. Graph paper, lined or dotted paper, cork board, and white or black boards are all choices now available in Flipgrid. In addition, split-screen recording is also available so the video recording can be on one side with the board on the other!	• Boards make it easy to share math lessons visually through the grid board, split screen, and more! • Use the split screen to create student vision boards, where students can set individual goals and share future dreams.
Photo Sticker	The custom image icon allows users to upload a picture in both .jpeg and .png formats. Images can be resized and added to the recording.	• Try creating your own custom frames for students to use by using .png files. • Use an uploaded photo as an anchor chart when creating tutorial or teaching videos for students.
GIF Sticker	Add elements of creativity with engaging GIFs that personalize a response.	• Capture character emotions or show points of view with various GIF stickers. • Stack GIFs on top of one another to create virtual scenes related to the topic of discussion. • Take advantage of GIF stickers (transparent backgrounds) to add characters into your video.
Upload Clip	Allows for app-smashing possibilities as you upload content created in other apps. Create or enhance in one tool, share, celebrate, and showcase in Flipgrid!	• Try recording an introduction on Flipgrid, then uploading a video. • Export a video created in a different app and upload it into Flipgrid.

No Audio	Deaf and hard of hearing learners or learners who are uncomfortable speaking can still share their voice in a way that works best for them. Simply record without audio. Learners can pair this feature with text + whiteboards + stickers to get creative results!	• Provides easy accessibility for learners who may not feel comfortable talking on camera. • Having a silent video often draws particular focus to the video content being shared.
Screen Recording	Not only can users record themselves, but they have the ability to screen record. Screen recording of the entire screen, a single window, or tab are all options given to the user, and you simply end the recording to go back to the original view.	• Create tutorials for a flipped classroom by screen recording directions and demonstrations for students ahead of time. • Model steps in a process for others to see and follow as many times as needed.
Pause Feature	Sometimes you start recording, and then need to stop to collect your thoughts. Users can start and stop the recording process as many times as they need, provided they are still under the required time.	• Try using the pause feature to create clever stop motion videos modeling concepts in science or to create an interview between characters. • After you press record, try pausing the video by clicking the spacebar. You can resume recording the same way, with less effort!
Video Editing	If you forget to mention something, you can always add it as a separate clip and then use Flipgrid's video editor to rearrange the clips.	• Gives students the option to record responses out of order and then allows them to move clips around. • Shorten the length of clips when there is unwanted time before or after recording. • Rotate the camera to get different camera views.

SIMPLE AND ENGAGING PLATFORM

The best tools are efficient and easy to use. In a classroom setting, a tool should also be kid friendly and appeal to their millennial mindset and social-learning loving, digital way of thinking. That's why Flipgrid is constantly working to simplify the learning experience and enhance engagement. Here are a few Flipgrid features that make this tool simple, engaging, and perfect for the classroom.

FLIPGRIDAR—FlipgridAR gives you the ability to place virtual elements in the physical world. The *AR* stands for *augmented reality*. With FlipgridAR, you can stick any Flipgrid video wherever you want by printing and posting its QR code for users to scan with either the Flipgrid mobile app or the QR scanner on any smartphone. This Flipgrid feature gives you the ability to transform family nights, homework, school events, book reviews, science fairs, student art galleries, language classrooms, *and more,* using FlipgridAR codes to instantly share videos featuring your students or yourself.

You can use this tool to share student voice by posting or sharing FlipgridAR codes to videos of your learners giving presentations about their classroom, their ideas, or their latest projects. Students and their families can watch videos as many times as they want or need to, which can be particularly helpful for learners who process best through verbal instruction. Simply record videos of yourself on Flipgrid to explain a lesson or assignment and share the FlipgridAR code so students and parents can watch and rewatch as needed.

> FlipgridAR is my favorite feature! I love that you can take anything basic and make it come to life. I enjoy using FlipgridAR to make so many interactive displays or directions! It makes using Flipgrid and collaborating across grade levels a breeze! I love seeing parents scan the QR code and seeing their reaction!
> —Jennifer Mahin (@jennasaurustech)

TOPIC VIEW—With the most recent updates, Flipgrid is now streamlined and organized for optimal viewer ease. Videos now have more space on the screen and will play right from this centralized view.

VIDEO PLAYER VIEW—When you click into a video, a modern design puts the student voice front and center. You can also see which video is "up next" to watch.

COMMENTS—Learners can reply to one another's videos with text and video, taking social learning to the next level. Educators can moderate, previewing any video or comment before activating it for everyone to see. With the use of advanced AI, Flipgrid scans for and filters out any bullying and toxic language to ensure that Flipgrid is a positive and fun experience for all. Your Topics will show a green checkmark as soon as you provide text or video feedback to students.

EDUCATOR COMMENTS—Educators can leave comments on videos in the form of a text or video. These comments can be made private, so only the individual learner can view, or public, so everyone in the Topic can view. The best part is that learners can view the comments right from the Topic in Flipgrid.

POWERFUL EDUCATOR DASHBOARD

When it comes to the Educator Dashboard, Flipgrid has worked tirelessly to create a platform that makes sharing Topics simple and easy. You can now start with a single Topic and centralize multiple discussions by adding Topics to a group! As a result, you don't always have to create a Group first.

TOPICS—In Flipgrid, a Topic is the conversation prompt or question, and it is the key to learners sharing their voice by recording a Flipgrid video. Topics can be shared to students as individual video tasks or as a part of a Group. Simply create your discussion prompt, choose how your community will access it, and then share! Topics are easy for educators to create with only two steps: Create your Topic and then choose who has access. All you need is a Topic to start quick discussions; you don't need to create a Group first. You can always move these Topics to Groups later if you choose or add a single Topic to multiple Groups.

GROUPS—Groups makes it easier for you to organize and share a collection of Topics with a group of learners. You can customize your group join code, add CoPilots, and more! You can create Groups before creating Topics, which is great when creating activities for a class, organizing a larger project or discussion, or when collaborating with students outside of your immediate classroom.

GUEST ACCESS—In addition to being able to add individual emails, you can set a Guest Password, which enables guests to join the conversation by using the same unique Topic code and then simply entering the password.

QUICKVIEW—Flipgrid makes it easy to review and share learner videos, reply with Comments, and edit Captions right from your Educator Dashboard.

ACCESSIBILITY

At the heart of every feature in Flipgrid is the idea of accessibility. It is part of Flipgrid's mission to create a platform that can be accessed and used by all learners. To that end, several embedded features make Flipgrid stand out from other education platforms. The following inclusive education tools give students personalized access to curriculum, optimize teacher time, and improve learning outcomes. As a result, Flipgrid allows students to grow their potential and gain independence while helping teachers feel more empowered to engage every learner.

IMMERSIVE READER—The Microsoft Immersive Reader is a free tool, built into Flipgrid, that implements proven techniques to improve reading and writing for people regardless of their age or ability. Students can access Microsoft's Immersive Reader on all text in Flipgrid. This powerful tool improves reading comprehension by offering dictation, decoding solutions, read-alouds, and real-time translation.

CLOSED CAPTIONS—If the closed captions feature is turned on, all Flipgrid videos are automatically transcribed and captioned by Microsoft Azure. Educators have the ability to edit captions as long the feature is turned on at the Topic level before recording. With this feature, you can make corrections and break up the transcript into appropriate, consumable chunks for your learners, and you can change the language. Note: Students can't edit their closed captions, but they can add custom text to their videos.

GAME CONTROLLER—This feature allows learners to use game controllers, including Xbox Adaptive Controller, to interact with the Flipgrid Camera.

ENRICHING COLLECTION OF READY-TO-USE ACTIVITIES

The Discovery Library is a great source to find and add Topics created by Flipgrid partners or other educators to your discussions. Ignite discussion with launch-ready, resource-packed, age- and subject-specific Topics from fellow educators around the world. Every Topic can be modified to meet the specific needs of your learners or simply launched as-is. The more than 25,000 different Topics housed in the Discovery Library can be filtered by subject area, by the age of your learners, or by the name of the educator who created it.

> My favorite feature of Flipgrid is the Discovery Library. I am able to search and add topics created by amazing educators who share their creativity with the Flipgrid community in order to benefit students around the world.
>
> —Stacy Benton (@sbentonteach)

COLLECTIONS—Collections allow you to explore an array of Topics within a specific subject or theme. Explore Collections such as Back to School; Conversations about Race, Equity, and Justice; or Conversation Starters for Topics to use with your learners. You can add Topics to create your own Collections. Create Collections organized by your subjects, languages, or your activities, or Topics submitted by other educators in your school. Share a Collection for other educators or CoPilots to use as well.

FEATURE TOPICS—Flipgrid highlights trending Topics and customizes the Topics you see first, based on your profile criteria.

PARTNER PAGES—Flipgrid proudly partners with organizations around the world to curate Topics. Explore Topics created by the Metropolitan Museum of Art to spark art discussions, support dyslexic learners with Made by Dyslexia, or empower learners to strive for diversity and inclusion with the Langston League. Partner pages contain all the information you need on each Flipgrid partner, such as their website and social accounts, as well as their Discovery

Library Collections. There are many unique partners to discover, including some of our favorites listed below:

- Langston League
- Made by Dyslexia
- Wonderopolis
- Epic
- Lego Education
- Capstone
- Nearpod
- BreakoutEDU
- Code.org
- Tynker
- KQED
- Adobe
- National WWII Museum
- Scholastic
- California State Parks
- Night Zoo Keeper
- North American Scholastic eSports Federation
- Decolonized
- Discovery Education
- The MET
- Buncee
- Find Your Grind
- Mote Marine Laboratory

USE THIS SPACE FOR SKETCH NOTES, IDEAS, ETC!

FLIPGRID INTEGRATIONS

Chapter 7

INTEGRATE *VERB*
/ˈin(t)əˌgrāt/
TO FORM, COORDINATE, OR BLEND INTO A FUNCTIONING OR
UNIFIED WHOLE

TheMerrillsEDU

You've heard of the old saying "two heads are better than one," right? Well, that adage is the one that comes to mind when we talk with educators about integrations. Integrations are at the heart of good edtech because they allow you to take advantage of the best features of two (or more) tools at once, creating a solution that is more powerful, engaging, and relevant than any single tool on its own.

You already know that Flipgrid is a powerful application and could be your single, go-to digital tool in the classroom. If you want to keep things simple, Flipgrid is robust enough to serve your students and their families both socially and academically. And if you like the idea of mixing things up and trying new things, integrations are another reason to love Flipgrid.

Flipgrid's developers work tirelessly to make it possible for teachers to include other learning platforms as part of the educational experience. They know that, by integrating other platforms, they can extend Flipgrid's reach and influence.

WHY BOTHER WITH INTEGRATIONS

Integrations are beneficial because educators can quickly and easily arrange content in multiple levels. This means that you (and your students) can use Flipgrid as your headquarters, even as you branch out and explore tools that may allow for different capabilities. Additionally, integrations can save time and money, expanding opportunities for all.

INTEGRATIONS SAVE TIME—One of the questions we are asked most frequently regarding how our students are able to navigate so many different apps and platforms in meaningful ways is, "Do they get lost?" Honestly, sometimes they do. And sometimes they get frustrated. But when applications can be integrated and work together, the propensity to get lost or frustrated is greatly diminished. Here's why: Integrations allow users to use a platform they are already familiar with and insert or add it to another, thus over time allowing them to be comfortable with both. With each new application they learn, their confidence grows, empowering them to branch out into more and more diverse platforms.

Integration creates equitable learning opportunities—Because it is free, Flipgrid automatically helps level the field, offering a space where all students and teachers can create, share, and discuss. With educational budgets constantly being limited or lowered, having access to a tool such as Flipgrid for free makes a big difference. In addition to the platform being free, many of the partners who share content on sites that otherwise charge subscriptions and fees give access to limited amounts of articles, games, and activities for free through Flipgrid's Discovery Library Topics and Collections.

When one app integrates with another, it allows you as the user to be more flexible while giving you the capability to create more. As much as we believe Flipgrid is the Swiss Army knife of education apps with all that it can do, there is undoubtedly going to be a time when you need students to be able to do something the platform either doesn't do or maybe doesn't do as efficiently. By integrating with other apps, Flipgrid gives students the ability to be more productive and efficient, while also branching out creatively with the content they are using to demonstrate their learning.

Flipgrid is an efficient platform in that it gives students the ability to create and house their work designed in other applications in addition to that filmed in Flipgrid. When you consider the tool's flexibility, which allows information to come into and flow out of it, Flipgrid easily becomes a foundational tool that is appropriate for any educational setting. Let's look at how Flipgrid allows for seamless integrations.

FLIPGRID INTEGRATIONS WITHIN OTHER PLATFORMS

In some cases, the type of learning you wish to foster in the classroom goes beyond pure discussion and video. For those lessons, Flipgrid makes it possible to take your Topics outside of their platform so you can integrate them with different programs and applications, some of which are listed below.

ANYWHERE—You can share a Flipgrid Topic, Group, or individual video anywhere! Simply grab the unique URL or embed code and paste it into any learning management system (LMS), website, email, or assignment.

NEARPOD—Flipgrid and Nearpod have teamed up to allow educators to embed Flipgrid Groups or Topics directly into Nearpod presentations. When creating your Nearpod presentation, simply add a new slide and choose Flipgrid from the Activities tab. To insert your Flipgrid Group or Topic, you will need to have both the student and teacher URLs ready to copy and paste. This means that you would first create the discussion in Flipgrid, then "embed" it into the Nearpod slide, using the links.

TEAMS—As part of the Microsoft family, Flipgrid integrates with other Microsoft 365 programs; for instance, Flipgrid can be added as a tab in Teams. Simply select Flipgrid on the top toolbar in Teams to make sparking a discussion quick and easy for any students working in that platform.

WAKELET—At the heart of Flipgrid is its amazing storytelling camera, and for this integration that's what was shared and embedded into Wakelet. When you are creating a new collection in Wakelet, the Flipgrid Camera is embedded in the Wakelet toolbar. Videos recorded in Wakelet are also stored in the Educator's Dashboard in Flipgrid under the Shorts tab, where it can be referred to or shared again if needed.

READ MORE ABOUT THIS INTEGRATION!

ONENOTE—Embedding Flipgrid into OneNote is a great way to deliver content to your students. To complete this process, click on the Share button from any Flipgrid Topic or Group. When the popup window opens, copy the URL. Then, click anywhere on your OneNote canvas and paste the URL. Your Flipgrid Topic or Group is then embedded into OneNote.

GOOGLE CLASSROOM—Sharing Flipgrid to Google Classroom is streamlined to just a few clicks. When you're ready to share a Topic with your students, click on the Share button from the Flipgrid Educator's Dashboard. Then, click the Google Classroom icon to open a set of options for your post.

READ MORE ABOUT THIS INTEGRATION!

FLIPGRID INTEGRATIONS WITHIN ITS OWN PLATFORM

When creating a Topic in Flipgrid, teachers can add enriching resources, including a video, photo, Microsoft Word, Google Docs, Wakelet collection, Adobe Spark, and more! In addition to a recorded or uploaded video, a YouTube link, image, GIF, or an emoji, educators also have the ability to embed content through special integrations with partners such as those listed below. That means when teachers create a new Topic for discussion or sharing, content from these partners can be displayed at the top as part of the first thing students see and use for their Flipgrid activity. Teachers have countless options and ways to transform their Topics based on the needs of individual classes and students.

BUNCEE—Create and share engaging content with students and pin this to the top of any Flipgrid topic. Whether this is a flipped lesson, an activity resource, or a learning visual, the pinned Buncee will be visible in real time.

ADOBE SPARK—Share a Spark web page, graphic, or video with your students. This integration allows you to make your Spark videos play right inside your Flipgrid Topics!

KAHOOT—Create an engaging and competitive game for students to participate in. First attach as a Topic focus, and when finished have students return to the Topic and reflect on the learning experience.

NEARPOD—Nearpod is known for its structured live lessons and student pacing lesson options. In addition to embedding Flipgrid topics into a Nearpod, educators also have the option of adding a Nearpod lesson as a focus in any Flipgrid Topic. Simply link any Nearpod lesson to the top of your Flipgrid Topic for students to easily access as part of the Flipgrid discussion.

NEWSELA—Discussions and debates about current events are at the heart of any reading and writing class. By integrating Newsela into Flipgrid, educators can pin any article or link directly from Newsela into the top of a Topic or Group.

WONDEROPOLIS—Wonderopolis is a resource full of articles and activities fueled by the curiosities and wonders of children. Attach a daily Wonder to a Topic to keep everything in one place when diving into the inquiry process and learning about something new and unusual.

GOOGLE—With a Google integration in Flipgrid, educators have the ability to extend learning experiences by providing students access to content via Docs, Sheets, Slides, and so forth in any Flipgrid Topic.

INTERACTIVE

FLIPGRID LESSONS

Flipgrid AR

TheMerrillsEDU

In true #interACTIVE fashion, we believe in the power of sharing ideas in the educator community. We all have talents, ideas, strengths, insights, and lessons that we can share with other educators to empower classroom and learning environments to be productive, inclusive, and engaging. We worked hard to ensure that this book is not just a reference but also a resource that you can take, use, and share with others.

In this section, we've included a wealth of lessons that we have created and used with our students and staff members. We are excited to share them with you and hope that you will find ways to incorporate them, tweak them, and build on them in your unique learning environments.

The lessons in this section start at the most at a basic level and gradually increase in difficulty or complexity regarding the setup, programs, and time involved. Many of the lessons have direct links to Topics in the Discovery Library that you can take and use today, in addition to resources and templates you can integrate directly into the Flipgrid Topics you create.

In an interACTIVE class, we believe it is important to infuse specific elements into lessons, so we have decided to visually represent these with the icons below. Each lesson is labeled with icons to show the specific components we believe are present in that particular lesson.

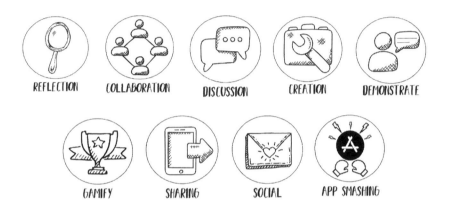

REFLECTION   COLLABORATION   DISCUSSION   CREATION   DEMONSTRATE

GAMIFY   SHARING   SOCIAL   APP SMASHING

I would highly recommend using Flipgrid in a learning environment with students of any age, as Flipgrid empowers all learners by providing them with a platform on which they can creatively express themselves and demonstrate their learning! With incredible features like filters, frames, emojis, text, boards, digital inking, photo stickers, and the ability to screen record, learners can creatively respond to provocations, reflection questions, or challenges Teachers provide as topics by sharing their ideas and opinions, as well as present written work or physical products and digital creations. Flipgrid is equally powerful for educators as it enables teachers to hear and see a student's depth of understanding and growth as a learner. Flipgrid can also be used to help students form connections and community both locally and globally. This not only gives students a more authentic experience in sharing their voices but also provides them with the opportunity to hear diverse perspectives, build open-mindedness, and develop empathy.

—Christine McKee (@CMcKee27)

FLIPGRID PLAYGROUND

PREP TIME:

COLLABORATION   DISCUSSION   REFLECTION   SHARING   SOCIAL

LESSON FORMAT: Teacher created

ACTIVITY DESCRIPTION: The playground is a place where students let their guard down and take a break from the academics in the classroom. Create a new Topic titled "Playground," where students can simply share cool things, hobbies, funny jokes, toys they like, and other nonacademic things with one another. This gives them a space to share about themselves and allows them to connect through common interests.

FEATURES USED: Flipgrid Camera, possibly moderation

TIPS AND TRICKS: It is a good idea to keep this Topic moderated at first so that the videos are viewed by the teacher before being published to the class.

GRAB THIS READY-TO-USE LESSON DIRECTLY FROM THE FLIPGRID DISCOVERY LIBRARY!

ALL ABOUT ME GRAFFITI

PREP TIME:

CREATION   DISCUSSION   SHARING   SOCIAL

LESSON FORMAT: Student created

ACTIVITY DESCRIPTION: Set aside a Topic in which students can share about themselves in a fun and artistic way. Using Topic Focus attachments, upload several brick walls for students to use as their own background when recording. Then have students take advantage of the amazing fonts and filters to create "graffiti" sharing all about themselves. When finished, students can voice over their artistic masterpieces, explaining all about themselves.

FEATURES USED: Topic Focus attachments, Text, Custom Sticker

TIPS AND TRICKS: Have students play with the text color, size and font style to mimic the look of real graffiti.

GRAB THIS READY-TO-USE LESSON DIRECTLY FROM THE FLIPGRID DISCOVERY LIBRARY!

SAY MY NAME

PREP TIME:

SHARING   REFLECTION   SOCIAL   DEMONSTRATE

LESSON FORMAT: Student created

ACTIVITY DESCRIPTION: Our names are part of our identity, so it is important to say our students' names correctly! Learn each child's name before the start of school by creating a topic for students to share their name and what makes their name special.

FEATURES USED: Flipgrid Camera, possibly FlipgridAR code or Topic QR code

TIPS AND TRICKS: Try creating this Topic ahead of the first day of school. Using the QR code features in Flipgrid, try attaching it to a teacher welcome postcard, or a back-to-school handout. This way students can respond and share before arriving on their first day, giving the teacher time to learn everyone's name ahead of time.

STUDENT SELFIES

PREP TIME:

CREATION   DISCUSSION   SOCIAL   SHARING   APP SMASHING

LESSON FORMAT: Student created

ACTIVITY DESCRIPTION: Taking selfies with the teacher on the first day of school is a staple for many elementary classrooms. Take fun .png frames and attach them in a simple Flipgrid Topic. Students can download the one they like, use it to take their first-day-of-school selfie, and then share with the class. They can even download their own video or selfie to keep as a classroom profile photo.

FEATURES USED: Custom Sticker, possibly Text

TIPS AND TRICKS: When designing, keep in mind the orientation students may be recording in depending on their device, and be sure to keep enough space open to leave room for the person recording the video to be seen.

GRAB SOME FREE FRAMES
TO GET STARTED!

LEVEL UP: We suggested designing in a program like Adobe Spark, because of the ability to save creations with a transparent background. After your frame has been designed, save the image as a .png file. Be sure to select "transparent background." This will take any of the white from the background layer and make it transparent.

MEET AND GREET

PREP TIME:

DISCUSSION SHARING

LESSON FORMAT: Student created

ACTIVITY DESCRIPTION: Face-to-face meet-and-greets with parents are great, but not everyone is able to participate or remember the information shared. By flipping your Meet-and-Greet and placing it as a Topic on your back-to-school Grid (use the Public/PLN Grid option), families can share a bit of their world and get to know you as well. It will introduce them to Flipgrid and let them have fun recording as a family!

FEATURES USED: Flipgrid Camera

TIPS AND TRICKS: If this is the first time the student and family will be using Flipgrid, make sure to explain that topics which are moderated won't show videos right away but rather once they are approved by the teacher.

BIRTHDAY MESSAGES

PREP TIME:

REFLECTION SOCIAL SHARING

LESSON FORMAT: Student created

ACTIVITY DESCRIPTION: It's always a good time to celebrate a birthday, and it's easy to do in Flipgrid! Set up a "Birthday" Group, and then create a Flipgrid Topic for each student. When their birthday arrives, have the class leave them a special message on the Topic. You could even have the class sing "Happy Birthday!"

FEATURES USED: Flipgrid Camera

TIPS AND TRICKS: You can plan ahead by creating a Flipgrid Topic for each student ahead of time, then keep the Topics "Hidden" so that they don't appear in what the students see. Then, when the big day comes, activate it, and it will be ready to go!

LEVEL UP: Share the link ahead of time with the students so family from both near and far can pop in and surprise students on their special day.

WHAT'S IN MY BAG

PREP TIME:

LESSON FORMAT: Student created

CREATION DISCUSSION SHARING SOCIAL APP SMASHING

ACTIVITY DESCRIPTION: Remember the old activity in which students had to go through and guess items from the teacher's bag, then listen to how each item revealed something about the teacher? Why not do this digitally with students? In the same way you would set up Student Selfies, attach the .png file frame of the bag for students within the topic, and then allow them to "add" things to their bag, filling it up with items that reveal something about themselves. Then they can share for their classmates to watch and learn more about them!

FEATURES USED: Custom Sticker, possibly text

LEVEL UP: Have students share their "bags" with images and words but no audio, so classmates can respond as they guess to whom each bag belongs.

GRAB THIS READY–TO–USE LESSON DIRECTLY FROM THE FLIPGRID DISCOVERY LIBRARY!

GUESS WHO FLIPGRID STYLE

PREP TIME:

LESSON FORMAT: Student created

DEMONSTRATE DISCUSSION GAMIFY CREATION

ACTIVITY DESCRIPTION: This fun take on a classic game is great for introducing new people or ideas. When recording the video, give clues to help viewers guess the person recording. When finished with the clues, use a sticker or image to hide the image of the person recording. Viewers then comment back with their guess as to who the person is.

FEATURES USED: Flipgrid Camera, Photo Sticker, Draw and Text Tools

TIPS AND TRICKS: Practice disguising your voice when recording, or don't use any audio at all! Instead, use the text features to write out the clues!

LEVEL UP: Try having students guess about academic topics. For example, students give three clues to describe a weekly vocabulary word using audio or text, and then the viewer has to comment with their guess of what word was being described. This could work for other academic topics such as Civil War battles, famous women activists, presidents, states and capitals, and much more!

GRAB THIS READY–TO–USE LESSON DIRECTLY FROM THE FLIPGRID DISCOVERY LIBRARY!

INFORMATION, FORMS, AND FAQS

PREP TIME:

COLLABORATION DISCUSSION SHARING

LESSON FORMAT: Teacher created

ACTIVITY DESCRIPTION: Do you have a list of forms parents need to complete or important information they need access to? Add your form or information as Topic attachments to your Welcome Back Flipgrid message to families. It serves as a great landing page to access important resources. Encourage families with questions to record a response to ask their question. It may be best to turn on "Response Moderation," and the questions you want to feature can become your school's FAQs.

FEATURES USED: Topic Media, Flipgrid Camera

TIPS AND TRICKS: Include the QR code for the Topic in newsletters, emails, or other first-week communications to help parents keep track of and find your information quickly and easily.

TEACHER'S ASSISTANT

PREP TIME:

DISCUSSION SHARING DEMONSTRATE

LESSON FORMAT: Teacher created

ACTIVITY DESCRIPTION: You can create a virtual teacher's assistant right within Flipgrid! Use the Flipgrid Camera to record yourself giving instructions, then download the QR code to the response. Print the QR code out and display it on the board. When students scan the QR code with the Flipgrid app, the video will appear in AR (augmented reality) so that they can listen to the expectations again rather than asking the teacher to repeat them. You can also include your Flipgrid video QR codes on newsletters to facilitate communication with families.

FEATURES USED: Flipgrid Camera, Flipgrid QR Code Reader (app)

TIPS AND TRICKS: Place the QR code on handouts before copying and include on virtual class websites or other digital assignments.

LEVEL UP: Instead of creating a Topic and QR code for every new activity and lesson, create one Topic titled "Teacher's Assistant." Use this "master" QR code on all assignments, simply swapping out the response videos based on the activities and lessons assigned that week. Use the Title feature when recording directions to clearly indicate which assignment the video directions correspond to.

CHECK OUR TUTORIAL VIDEO TO GET STARTED!

OFFICE HOURS

PREP TIME:

COLLABORATION DISCUSSION SHARING

LESSON FORMAT: Teacher created

ACTIVITY DESCRIPTION: Create a "virtual office" with Flipgrid, where students and families can communicate with you via "video voicemail." Moderating the conversation will keep it private, and you can turn on email notifications to alert you when a new video has been posted. Then you can respond appropriately in a timely manner.

FEATURES USED: Flipgrid Camera

TIPS AND TRICKS: Create a sign to hang on a classroom or office door that includes the sharable QR code that when scanned will link directly to the Topic.

MORNING MEETING

PREP TIME:

REFLECTION DEMONSTRATE SOCIAL SHARING

LESSON FORMAT: Teacher created

ACTIVITY DESCRIPTION: Give students the chance to share about themselves and express their thoughts and feelings in a group setting either virtually or in person. Set up a Morning Meeting Topic for students to share around a specific theme or question, such as "What makes us all unique?" or "How can we show kindness at school?"

FEATURES USED: Flipgrid Camera

TIPS AND TRICKS: Make sure to give students time not only to record their ideas, but also to view the ideas of others and comment back accordingly.

WOULD YOU RATHER

DISCUSSION DEMONSTRATE REFLECTION GAMIFY

PREP TIME:

LESSON FORMAT: Teacher and Student Created

ACTIVITY DESCRIPTION: Spark conversation and even debate by using a would-you-rather format question using Flipgrid. Create a Topic with this would-you-rather question; students can then explain their reasoning in their video response.

FEATURES USED: Flipgrid Camera, other features such as split screen, text, inking

TIPS AND TRICKS: Try starting with this fun Discovery Library topic for math!

GRAB THIS READY-TO-USE LESSON DIRECTLY FROM THE FLIPGRID DISCOVERY LIBRARY!

CHECK-IN SESSION

PREP TIME:

REFLECTION SHARING SOCIAL

LESSON FORMAT: Teacher created

ACTIVITY DESCRIPTION: Create a private space for your students to share their feelings via Flipgrid. The goal here is to provide an outlet for your students to vent and for you to listen; that way you gain an even better understanding of what is happening in their day. Be sure to enable moderation to keep discussion between you and the student.

FEATURES USED: Flipgrid Camera, other tools as needed

TIPS AND TRICKS: Try sharing the QR code on a sign displayed somewhere in the room so students can access it easily when needed. The same QR code could also be used to create small student cards or badges to have with them at all times (even at home!) if they feel the need to share something with the teacher.

GRAB THIS READY-TO-USE LESSON DIRECTLY FROM THE FLIPGRID DISCOVERY LIBRARY!

ROCK, PAPER, SCISSORS!

PREP TIME:

COLLABORATION GAMIFY SHARING

LESSON FORMAT: Student created

ACTIVITY DESCRIPTION: Build your classroom community and encourage honesty with this fun spin on the traditional game. Have your students record themselves saying, "Rock, paper, scissors…" and then share what they picked. Their friends can watch the videos back and participate "virtually" (without cheating, of course!) and reply with what they selected and whether they were defeated—again encouraging honesty!

FEATURES USED: Flipgrid Camera

TIPS AND TRICKS: If you're worried about students cheating, have them choose a Flipgrid response to reply to. Instruct them to not watch the original video before responding. Then, after the second student has left a response, they can go back and leave another response indicating whether they won or lost the match.

GRAB THIS READY-TO-USE LESSON DIRECTLY FROM THE FLIPGRID DISCOVERY LIBRARY!

LEVEL UP: IF YOU'D LIKE TO INCORPORATE THIS ACTIVITY WITH A FUN READ-ALOUD, WE LOVE THE BOOK THE LEGEND OF ROCK PAPER SCISSORS BY DREW DAYWALT.

TALENT SHOW

PREP TIME:

CREATION   SHARING   DEMONSTRATE

LESSON FORMAT: Student created

ACTIVITY DESCRIPTION: Let your students' talent shine by providing them a space to share their passions. This is a great way to discover something new about your students that they may not normally get to share in the classroom. For example, let your students share their musical talent, a new dance, or share a "trick shot" for the rest of the class (or world) to see.

FEATURES USED: Flipgrid Camera

TIPS AND TRICKS: Once all students have shared a response, select them all and create a MixTape to share with families.

LEVEL UP: Create a schoolwide talent show with entries from students in various grades. This is a great way to build community with students regardless of their individual teacher or grade level.

FLIPGRID SPELLING

PREP TIME:

REFLECTION   DEMONSTRATE

LESSON FORMAT: Teacher created

ACTIVITY DESCRIPTION: If you're looking for an easy way to practice spelling, try assigning your students this task in Flipgrid. Record yourself going through the words you would like your students to practice spelling (be sure not to spell them!). Have your students respond by spelling out each word.

FEATURES USED: Flipgrid Camera

TIPS AND TRICKS: Teach your students that when they practice the spelling of the words, they can respond directly to themselves to keep their responses organized in one thread. This way it's easier for you to monitor their progress.

RUNNING RECORDS AND FLUENCY CHECKS

PREP TIME:

COLLABORATION   DISCUSSION   SHARING

LESSON FORMAT: Teacher created

ACTIVITY DESCRIPTION: Finding the time to sit and individually listen to every student in the class read can be overwhelming and take a lot of class time to carry out. Attach the reading passage to a Flipgrid Topic and have students access it on their own, reading aloud to the teacher in their video response. Then use the moderate video feature to leave responses hidden for only the teacher to see!

FEATURES USED: Topic Media, Flipgrid Camera

TIPS AND TRICKS: If you are timing how many words a student can read, try cutting the recording time off at that time to help when reviewing student videos. This way the video will end at the exact time, making it easier to count words and find where the student ended reading.

GRAB THIS READY-TO-USE
LESSON DIRECTLY FROM
THE FLIPGRID
DISCOVERY LIBRARY!

ADVICE FOR NEXT YEAR'S CLASS

PREP TIME:

REFLECTION   SOCIAL   SHARING

LESSON FORMAT: Student created

ACTIVITY DESCRIPTION: As the class reflects on the school year, have them share their advice for the new students coming to that grade level next year. These videos can then be saved and used when the new students arrive after summer break. They are an easy, nonthreatening way for students to get to know their new teacher, classroom, and maybe even school without having to feel embarrassed or awkward asking lots of questions.

FEATURES USED: Flipgrid Camera, other tools as needed

TIPS AND TRICKS: Giving students ideas on what to talk about may help kickstart the conversations. Questions regarding classroom procedures, school expectations, or quirky teacher likes and dislikes are always fun to start with.

LEVEL UP: Connect with your local middle or high school and have them work to create connections with the students who are moving up to the new school.

FICTION OR NONFICTION

PREP TIME:

DEMONSTRATE   REFLECTION   DISCUSSION   CREATION   SHARING

LESSON FORMAT: Student created

ACTIVITY DESCRIPTION: Have your students illustrate an imaginary book cover on a sheet of paper or on any creation platform. When finished, have students share their book cover in the Topic while challenging their classmates to guess whether they think the book cover would be fiction or nonfiction. After a select amount of time, allow the illustrators time to go back and respond to their video's replies.

FEATURES USED: Flipgrid Camera

CHECK OUT OUR TWEET!

LEVEL UP: If you're working with older learners, allow them to design a fake blog post or fake social media post. Give students a book template image to upload on Flipgrid using the Custom Sticker feature, and allow them to create using the tools within the Flipgrid camera.

STAFF INTRODUCTIONS

PREP TIME:

SOCIAL   SHARING

LESSON FORMAT: Teacher created

ACTIVITY DESCRIPTION: Keep your school community connected all year long with Staff Introductions in Flipgrid. Using the Flipgrid Camera, educators can introduce themselves and discuss some of their favorite things. Once you have all the responses collected, embed the Group onto your school's website or share the link on social media. Families can learn more about your educators before you even open the campus for the school year.

FEATURES USED: Flipgrid Camera

TIPS AND TRICKS: Several features will allow personalization in the responses. For example, try adding text to a selfie. If an educator has forgotten to add their name in a Flipgrid response, you can always go back and edit it for them from the educator's dashboard.

LEVEL UP: This activity could also be done with a new class, cohort, or grade level of students. Try having upcoming fifth graders introduce themselves to each other.

BOOK SNAPS

PREP TIME:

DEMONSTRATE   DISCUSSION   REFLECTION   CREATION

LESSON FORMAT: Student created

ACTIVITY DESCRIPTION: Book Snaps are photographs from a page in a book where students can highlight important parts or share their thinking at certain points in the text. Have your students capture a photograph from any text and upload it as a Photo Sticker. Resize and move the image as necessary. They can use the Draw tool to annotate the text (underline, highlight), along with the Text tool, according to the given assignment. Finally, they can record a video next to the Photo Sticker (or enlarge the Book Snap to take up the entire screen) as they share their voice.

FEATURES USED: Flipgrid Camera, Photo Sticker, Draw and Text Tools

TIPS AND TRICKS: When working with younger students, try providing the image of the text you want students to use. This will help save time while teaching the process to students for the first time.

3 EMOJI SUMMARY

PREP TIME:

DISCUSSION   DEMONSTRATE   CREATION   REFLECTION   GAMIFY

LESSON FORMAT: Student created

ACTIVITY DESCRIPTION: After reading a text, have your students create a Flipgrid video that uses the emoji stickers to summarize the story. For example, have the students use a different emoji for the beginning, middle, and end. Then, have the students explain why they chose the emoji that they did to provoke higher-level thinking skills.

FEATURES USED: Flipgrid Camera, Stickers

TIPS AND TRICKS: This same activity can be done using a sheet of paper for the emojis. Have the students draw the emoji of their choice on the paper, repeat as needed, then share the illustration in a Flipgrid video. This provides an artistic outlet, and it is great for "littles," who may need to stop at various points of the text so they don't lose focus.

CHECK OUR TUTORIAL VIDEO TO GET STARTED!

ENCOURAGEMENT FROM HOME

PREP TIME:

SOCIAL   SHARING

LESSON FORMAT: Teacher created

ACTIVITY DESCRIPTION: Have families record videos for their children to provide encouragement from home. Don't just wait for testing time to have your families record videos. The beginning of the year, at parent conferences, or a sendoff to the next grade are all ways to get families involved in encouraging and supporting their kids.

FEATURES USED: Flipgrid Camera, other tools as needed

TIPS AND TRICKS: This can be fun to do before big events such as state testing, but it is also easy to integrate into special events such as the first day of school, student-led conferences, or other big events occurring both in and out of the classroom.

GRAB THIS READY-TO-USE
LESSON DIRECTLY FROM
THE FLIPGRID
DISCOVERY LIBRARY!

PE TRAINING VIDEOS

PREP TIME:

REFLECTION   DEMONSTRATE

LESSON FORMAT: Teacher created

ACTIVITY DESCRIPTION: Use the Flipgrid Camera to record a demonstration of how a physical education activity is to be performed.

FEATURES USED: Flipgrid Camera

TIPS AND TRICKS: Be sure to take advantage of pausing/recording when creating your videos. This will make understanding the directions easier for students.

FLIPGRID VOICEMAIL

PREP TIME:

SHARING   SOCIAL

LESSON FORMAT: Teacher created

ACTIVITY DESCRIPTION: Create a Topic where students and families can leave you messages. This works perfectly if your students or families need help with assignments after hours, or if there's a situation in which the teacher is unavailable.

FEATURES USED: Flipgrid Camera

TIPS AND TRICKS: Try this idea if you're planning to be off campus with a substitute for an extended amount of time!

FLIPGRID TV CHANNELS

PREP TIME:

LESSON FORMAT: Teacher created

ACTIVITY DESCRIPTION: Providing students choices is easy with Flipgrid. Create "channels" designed with tasks for your students to complete. Create a Flipgrid Topic, then save it. Log on to the Topic as if you were a student, and post the number of "channels" (or activities) that you would like them to complete. Be sure to use your favorite Flipgrid feature to add a channel number, or indicate it in the title.

FEATURES USED: Flipgrid Camera, Photo Stickers, Filters

TIPS AND TRICKS: Scan the QR code to see our demonstration of how you can upload a TV Photo Sticker and use the filters to make it appear as though you are really inside a television!

GET STARTED HERE!

LEVEL UP: Attach the .png image in the Topic Focus and have your students answer back with their own "channel" responses.

CLASSROOM TOUR

PREP TIME:

LESSON FORMAT: Teacher created

ACTIVITY DESCRIPTION: Starting a new school year in a new and unfamiliar classroom can be intimidating and scary for many students. Give students a firsthand view of the classroom through a tour on Flipgrid. Take the time to point out different areas in the room and where supplies and materials are located. Send the tour home to students before the first day of school by using the sharable link or QR code.

FEATURES USED: Flipgrid Camera

LEVEL UP: Give students a schoolwide tour by creating a topic with several video responses. Share spaces such as the media center or library, cafeteria, playground, and so forth, giving a tour of the space while also sharing procedures and expectations for when they are in each location. Freeze the Topic before sharing with families so no further changes can be made.

SIGHT WORDS

PREP TIME:

LESSON FORMAT: Teacher created

ACTIVITY DESCRIPTION: Help your "littles" master their sight words with this easily differentiated activity. Record yourself going through a set of your sight words. We recommend starting a new Topic for each set; that way you can differentiate who receives them. Share the appropriate Topic code with the student(s). They can watch the video and practice the words at their own pace.

FEATURES USED: Flipgrid Camera

TIPS AND TRICKS: When recording your sight word videos, be sure to record each set as its own Topic. You may want to enable the captions so that your students can see and read the word(s) as they appear on the screen.

CHECK OUR TUTORIAL
VIDEO TO GET STARTED!

TWO TRUTHS AND A LIE

PREP TIME:

DISCUSSION   SOCIAL   SHARING   GAMIFY

LESSON FORMAT: Student created

ACTIVITY DESCRIPTION: Gamify getting to know your students at the beginning of the year with this simple, yet fun activity. Create a Flipgrid Topic where your students share about themselves by revealing two truths and one lie. The key is they don't reveal which statement is the lie! Give classmates time to try and guess which statement is the lie. Looking for something more academic? Swap out your students with characters from a book, or historical figures.

FEATURES USED: Flipgrid Camera

LEVEL UP: Take this to next level by using it in a more academic setting. Have students create true and false statements based on content read and learned in class. Students must identify the false statements of their classmates and reply to them, using evidence from the text.

GRAB THIS READY-TO-USE
LESSON DIRECTLY FROM
THE FLIPGRID
DISCOVERY LIBRARY!

STUDENT OF THE WEEK

PREP TIME:

REFLECTION   SOCIAL   SHARING

LESSON FORMAT: Student created

ACTIVITY DESCRIPTION: Have each student record a video sharing why the Student of the Week is special. Students will enjoy watching video messages from their classmates sharing why they are valued members of their classroom community.

FEATURES USED: Flipgrid Camera, other tools as needed

TIPS AND TRICKS: Use the Topic video as a space for the teacher to start the discussion by sharing about this students and modeling for their classmates the types of comments and ideas to share.

LEVEL UP: Highlight students at a schoolwide level for things like Do the Right Thing Awards or Character Month, where multiple students are highlighted. Share with parents in a schoolwide email or newsletter using the share link or QR sharing feature.

GRAB THIS READY-TO-USE LESSON DIRECTLY FROM THE FLIPGRID DISCOVERY LIBRARY!

UNDERCOVER SPY IN FLIPGRID

PREP TIME:

DISCUSSION   CREATION   GAMIFY

LESSON FORMAT: Student created

ACTIVITY DESCRIPTION: Become an undercover spy in Flipgrid! Use this for simple activities such as having littles look for clues in a text, use it with middle school students as they observe and analyze steps in a science experiment, or even have high schoolers use it when responding to and debating historical events such as Watergate or the assassination of JFK. Using a filter and GIF Stickers from the Flipgrid Effects creates a secret undercover video appearance that is engaging for all!

FEATURES USED: Flipgrid Camera, Filters, GIFs (Stickers)

TIPS AND TRICKS: Try using the DuoTone Flipgrid filter for a "night vision" look, or the "Black and White" filter for a "security camera" look.

GET STARTED HERE!

ART SHOWCASE

PREP TIME:

REFLECTION   SOCIAL   SHARING

LESSON FORMAT: Student created

ACTIVITY DESCRIPTION: Share the artist alongside the art with FlipgridAR! Before hanging up a piece of art to share, have students record a video response explaining their art, the technique used to create it, and anything else relevant to the project. Print the FlipgridAR code and hang it alongside the art so others can get to know the face behind the work!

FEATURES USED: FlipgridAR

TIPS AND TRICKS: Create a direction sign to hang near art for those viewing who may be new to Flipgrid or unsure of how to view videos.

LEVEL UP: Create a Mixtape playlist of all the videos to send home so parents and family who can't see the art in person can also view the work.

GRAB THIS READY-TO-USE LESSON DIRECTLY FROM THE FLIPGRID DISCOVERY LIBRARY!

POETRY SLAM

PREP TIME:

DISCUSSION   CREATION   SHARING

LESSON FORMAT: Student created

ACTIVITY DESCRIPTION: Sharing written work can be hard for many students, so give them a chance to do so using Flipgrid! Have students share their poems and then watch in live feed one after the other to create a virtual poetry slam!

FEATURES USED: Flipgrid Camera

TIPS AND TRICKS: If students don't want to share their face, allow them to be creative with the text and board tools.

CHARACTER CHARADES

PREP TIME:

CREATION   REFLECTION   DEMONSTRATE

LESSON FORMAT: Student created

ACTIVITY DESCRIPTION: Tie this Flipgrid activity into the popular book, "Parker Looks Up." After reading the story, have the students create a Flipgrid video where they describe the characters from the story. Have them take advantage of Flipgrid's emoji stickers by adding a pirate hat and sunglasses to match the same items described in the story (click: effects, emoji–then search for hat and sunglasses).

FEATURES USED: Flipgrid Camera, Drawing

CHECK OUT OUR TWEET!

CUBE CONSTRUCTION

PREP TIME:

LESSON FORMAT: Teacher created

DISCUSSION   REFLECTION   DEMONSTRATE   GAMIFY

ACTIVITY DESCRIPTION: Pre-record six Topic videos ahead of time and print out the QR code images for each one. The Topic videos can be asking students questions, proposed exit ticket activities, or comprehension questions pertaining to a specific passage of text. Once the six QR codes are printed, cut them out and tape them together to form a cube that students can then roll on the table and use to engage with the Topics.

FEATURES USED: Topic QR codes

TIPS AND TRICKS: Try leaving multiple tasks for students in each Topic so they can keep interacting with it if they roll that QR code more than once.

GET STARTED HERE!

ANCHOR CHARTS IN A FLIPPED CLASSROOM

PREP TIME:

LESSON FORMAT: Teacher created

DEMONSTRATE   DISCUSSION

ACTIVITY DESCRIPTION: Take flipped lessons to the next level by attaching an anchor chart to your Flipgrid videos! Start by taking a photo of the anchor chart, or recreate it digitally and save it to your device. Upload the image using the Photo Sticker feature. Resize the image as needed, and then hit record!

FEATURES USED: Flipgrid Camera, Text, Stickers, Photo Stickers

TIPS AND TRICKS: When resizing your anchor charts, try going for a split screen—½ anchor chart, ½ video. Then you can record yourself talking right next to the anchor chart!

GET STARTED HERE!

FLIPMOJI MATH

PREP TIME:

DISCUSSION   DEMONSTRATE   CREATION   GAMIFY

LESSON FORMAT: Teacher or Student created

ACTIVITY DESCRIPTION: Use the Stickers found in the Flipgrid Camera to create a math scenario. Start out with using two of the same stickers and have them equal a different sticker (for example: happy face + happy face = car). Then, start another line using one of each of the previous stickers to equal a third new sticker (for example, happy face + car = sun). Repeat this process as many times as you would like. The goal for the students is to figure out the value of each sticker.

FEATURES USED: Flipgrid Camera, Stickers

LEVEL UP: This doesn't have to be a teacher-created lesson! Let your students design their own Flipmoji Math scenarios so they can challenge their classmates!

CHECK OUR TUTORIAL
VIDEO TO GET STARTED!

SHOW AND TELL

PREP TIME:

DISCUSSION   SOCIAL   SHARING

LESSON FORMAT: Student created

ACTIVITY DESCRIPTION: Create a Flipgrid Topic for your students to show and tell all about something unique. This is a great way to get to know your students on a different level, because they can complete the task from home. Classmates can then respond, making connections to one another, thus building a stronger classroom community.

FEATURES USED: Flipgrid Camera

TIPS AND TRICKS: We suggest moderating this Flipgrid Topic; in other words, once a video is submitted, you (the educator) will be notified. Each video will not appear for students until you have approved it. Note: All replies will also need to be approved.

HONEY, I SHRUNK THE TEACHER!

PREP TIME:

LESSON FORMAT: Teacher created

COLLABORATION   DEMONSTRATE   CREATION   GAMIFY   APP SMASHING

ACTIVITY DESCRIPTION: Recreate the classic 80s film, *Honey I Shrunk the Kids*, with a twist! Use "Scenes" in the app Apple Clips and select "Backyard." This will place you in a scene with an AR background. Record a challenge for your students where they have to rescue you and return you back to normal size. Save the video and upload it to Flipgrid. Have the students solve the challenge and share their thinking.

FEATURES USED: Flipgrid Camera, Appsmash with Apple Clips

TIPS AND TRICKS: Try creating multiple challenges in Apple Clips, then upload them to Flipgrid as though you are a student. If you have multiple challenges, keep everything "Hidden" except for the first challenge. Tell your students to respond directly back to you (instead of adding a new video); this will keep the thread organized. When students start answering correctly, unlock the next challenge by toggling the second challenge from "Hidden" to "Active."

CHECK OUR TUTORIAL
VIDEO TO GET STARTED!

READING FLUENCY CHECK

PREP TIME:

LESSON FORMAT: Student created

REFLECTION   DEMONSTRATE

ACTIVITY DESCRIPTION: Create a Topic where your students can record themselves reading from a passage or text. Explain to them that they are to read until the video runs out of time. This gives the teacher a video of the student reading and can be used to check fluency.

FEATURES USED: Flipgrid Camera

TIPS AND TRICKS: We recommend creating a Group to organize the texts that you are assigning. For example, create a Group for Reading Fluency, and then build Topics so that the students can quickly find them.

GRAB THIS READY-TO-USE
LESSON DIRECTLY FROM
THE FLIPGRID
DISCOVERY LIBRARY!

SUMMARIZING STORIES

PREP TIME:

LESSON FORMAT: Student created

COLLABORATION   REFLECTION   DEMONSTRATE   CREATION   GAMIFY

ACTIVITY DESCRIPTION: Have your students become newscasters! Use the Flipgrid Camera to record a video that summarizes a story. When ready to record, click on the Flipgrid Frames and use the "Breaking News" frame. Now your students are news reporters who can quickly summarize the main idea!

FEATURES USED: Flipgrid Camera, Frames

LEVEL UP: Have students interview one another in the same video to get different perspectives!

GRAB THIS READY-TO-USE LESSON DIRECTLY FROM THE FLIPGRID DISCOVERY LIBRARY!

VIRTUAL FIELD TRIPS

PREP TIME:

LESSON FORMAT: Teacher created

REFLECTION   SHARING   APP SMASHING

ACTIVITY DESCRIPTION: Reach out to field trip destinations and invite the staff to participate in a virtual field trip! This is a great way to follow up field trips with any questions that you might have. It's also a great way to reach destinations that you are unable to visit. Curate resources from the destination, then share them on Flipgrid and allow your students the opportunity to ask questions in a Topic.

FEATURES USED: Flipgrid Camera

TIPS AND TRICKS: Be sure to check the Discovery Library for virtual field trips that have already been created!

GRAB THIS READY-TO-USE LESSON DIRECTLY FROM THE FLIPGRID DISCOVERY LIBRARY!

LIVING VS. NON-LIVING

PREP TIME:

LESSON FORMAT: Student created

CREATION   REFLECTION   DEMONSTRATE

ACTIVITY DESCRIPTION: Students can take advantage of the Flipgrid app and head outside looking for living and nonliving things. While recording, as students identify examples of living and non-living things they are able to draw or ink live on the video.

FEATURES USED: Flipgrid Camera, Drawing

LEVEL UP: Students can "hunt" and look for all sorts of things depending on their grade level or subject area. Try identifying shapes in nature, arrays in the classroom, or patterns in everyday objects.

GRAB THIS READY-TO-USE LESSON DIRECTLY FROM THE FLIPGRID DISCOVERY LIBRARY!

MATH EXPLANATIONS

PREP TIME:

LESSON FORMAT: Teacher and Student created

SHARING   SOCIAL   GAMIFY   APP SMASHING

COLLABORATION   DEMONSTRATE   DISCUSSION   CREATION   REFLECTION

ACTIVITY DESCRIPTION: Give students a platform not only for providing answers to math problems but also a place where they can explain their thinking by using the Flipgrid Camera. Students can use various tools to visually show how they solved the problem and collaborate with others who may have solved differently. This provides an opportunity for students to view multiple strategies, rather than observing only the teacher directly.

FEATURES USED: Text Tool, Split Screen, Boards

LEVEL UP: Try app smashing with Wakelet, where students can respond with a "written" or typed explanation of their math along with a Shorts video embedded inside. This will create a curation of student explanations in one free-flowing thread.

LISTENING COMPREHENSION

PREP TIME:

LESSON FORMAT: Teacher and Student Created

DEMONSTRATE   REFLECTION

ACTIVITY DESCRIPTION: Use the Flipgrid Camera to record yourself reading from a text or article. After you have finished reading, challenge the students by asking questions to monitor their listening comprehension. The students can then respond in a Flipgrid video explaining their thinking.

FEATURES USED: Flipgrid Camera

TIPS AND TRICKS: If you're reading from a longer text, we recommend creating a Group; you can continue to add Topics into it. This way, you can keep all student responses from that particular piece of literature together (and the content may be revisited easily in an organized fashion).

PAPER SLIDES

PREP TIME:

LESSON FORMAT: Student created

COLLABORATION REFLECTION DEMONSTRATE CREATION

ACTIVITY DESCRIPTION: Have your students use blank sheets of paper to illustrate their thinking, or describe a figure or location. Hold the illustrations up one-by-one in front of the Flipgrid Camera. Record a quick segment, then tap the pause button. Swap out the first illustration with the next one and follow the same procedure. Repeat this process as many times as needed!

FEATURES USED: Flipgrid Camera

TIPS AND TRICKS: After you click the record button, you can use the spacebar to pause the recording. Using this key helps make the video transition quickly and smoothly.

CHECK OUT OUR TWEET!

ROLL THE DICE

PREP TIME:

LESSON FORMAT: Teacher created

DISCUSSION DEMONSTRATE GAMIFY

ACTIVITY DESCRIPTION: Use Flipgrid to take the ordinary lesson of answering comprehension questions to the next level. Assign questions to different digits up to 12 and then have students roll the dice to determine which questions they are to answer in the Flipgrid Topic. The teacher prerecords Topic responses for each of the questions, and when students roll and then go to respond, they comment under the teacher video response for that question.

FEATURES USED: Flipgrid Camera

TIPS AND TRICKS: Make sure students comment under each teacher response video, so all responses to that question are organized accordingly.

CHECK OUR TUTORIAL
VIDEO TO GET STARTED!

DIGITAL CAREER DAY

PREP TIME:

DISCUSSION   SHARING

LESSON FORMAT: Teacher created

ACTIVITY DESCRIPTION: Create a Flipgrid Topic and invite members of the community to share their expertise. Students can watch the videos and then leave them any questions that they might have. These conversations can grow and continue over a few days or an extended length of time, giving students a chance to learn more and interact more closely with the "expert."

FEATURES USED: Flipgrid Camera, other features such as Topic attachments in video

TIPS AND TRICKS: Provide your guests with a "Guest Password" to provide easy access into your Topic.

GRAB THIS READY-TO-USE LESSON DIRECTLY FROM THE FLIPGRID DISCOVERY LIBRARY!

TECH TUTORIAL HOTLINE

PREP TIME:

CREATION   DEMONSTRATE

LESSON FORMAT: Teacher or Student created

ACTIVITY DESCRIPTION: Create a Group where you or your students can provide tutorials in Topics. These tutorials can be used to share with each other, share with families, or to train your students on how to use new technology.

FEATURES USED: Flipgrid Camera

TIPS AND TRICKS: Try using Flipgrid's Screen Recording to capture video tutorials from a desktop to model more.

LEVEL UP: Take these explanations to the next level by prerecording them and taking the Topic QR codes and attaching them to paper practice sheets before copying. This will provide students with built-in help in case they need it!

MANIPULATIVE MATH

PREP TIME:

LESSON FORMAT: Teacher created

ACTIVITY DESCRIPTION: This activity can be done as an educator or as a student. When designing a Flipgrid video as an educator, use the Flipgrid Stickers as manipulatives to help viewers understand the content. Students can do the same, explaining their thinking and moving the Stickers around while the video is recording.

FEATURES USED: Flipgrid Camera, Stickers, Draw, Board

TIPS AND TRICKS: Try recording short segments. Start by recording yourself, then use Flipgrid's Board feature to fill the video screen. When planning, if you need numerous Stickers for your video, duplicate the Stickers on top of one another. That way you can easily click and drag them without having to press pause and record.

CHECK OUR TUTORIAL
VIDEO TO GET STARTED!

DIGITAL BREAKOUT

PREP TIME:

LESSON FORMAT: Teacher created

ACTIVITY DESCRIPTION: Set up a new private Group. Edit the name appropriately, and then change the join code to the answer of a clue (for example, if you were trying to get your students to solve 600 + 600, change the join code to 1,200). Then, click the option to add student usernames. Create a "fake" student name, and then enter a username that is the answer to the second challenge (For example, if the next challenge you want the students to complete is 1,200 − 300, the students would need to enter "900" to gain access.). When you have everything ready, share out the original Group code with the students. Let them work through each challenge, and once they are able to solve all challenges, they can leave a victory message!

FEATURES USED: Flipgrid Camera

TIPS AND TRICKS: If you have students who are unable to log in, you will know that they are struggling with the concepts!

CHECK OUR TUTORIAL
VIDEO TO GET STARTED!

BOOK CLUBS/READ-ALOUD

PREP TIME:

DISCUSSION   REFLECTION   SHARING

LESSON FORMAT: Teacher created

ACTIVITY DESCRIPTION: Create a Topic for your read-aloud, and encourage students to leave questions or ideas from the story in videos. This can be used in Literature Circles, where you assign different tasks to students throughout each chapter of the story.

FEATURES USED: Flipgrid Camera

TIPS AND TRICKS: If you're working with multiple books, try creating a Group for each story. Doing so will easily differentiate your instruction!

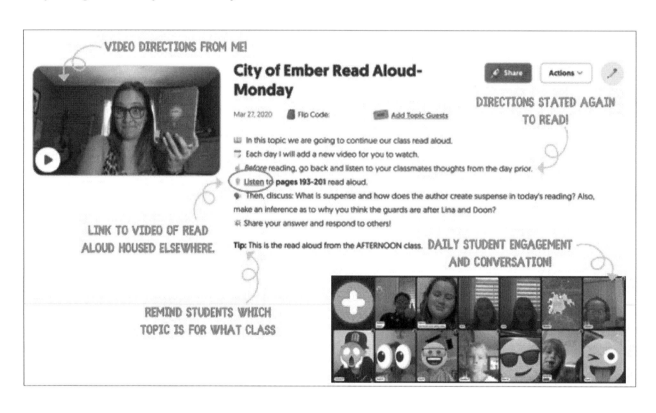

> Experiment with a small assignment first and then build up to where kids respond to each other. Flipgrid is a great way for kids to communicate ideas, thoughts, and for some, it motivates them to speak for the first time ever in their life.
>
> —Lester Dinerstein (@mrdsengclasss)

SPEED DEBATING

PREP TIME:

LESSON FORMAT: Teacher or Student created

DISCUSSION   REFLECTION   DEMONSTRATE

ACTIVITY DESCRIPTION: Spice up the idea of an old debate by having students "speed debate" their ideas, using Flipgrid. Instead of roaming the room to debate ideas or reasoning, students can share these ideas together in one Topic. The teacher can set up the topics for debate ahead of time for students to comment and reply to as well.

FEATURES USED: Flipgrid Camera

TIPS AND TRICKS: Encourage students to try to respond to as many different views in a specific amount of time, to encourage the sharing of ideas in a short amount of time, like speed debating.

MY TEACHER . . . STUCK IN MINECRAFT!

PREP TIME:

LESSON FORMAT: Teacher created

REFLECTION   DISCUSSION   CREATION   GAMIFY   DEMONSTRATE

ACTIVITY DESCRIPTION: Turn your classroom into a Minecraft World with Flipgrid's "Pixel" or "Brick" filter. Think of a creative challenge for your students. Set up a Topic for the challenge. Start off recording as a student without a filter, then click the pause button and toggle the "Pixel" or "Brick" filter. Then proceed with recording. This will allow you to go from normal to pixelated. Submit the challenge, then repeat if needed. When your students log on to the Topic, they will be faced with your Minecraft challenges!

FEATURES USED: Flipgrid Camera, Filters

TIPS AND TRICKS: If you have multiple challenges, keep everything "Hidden" except for the first challenge. Tell your students to respond directly back to you (instead of adding a new video); this will keep the thread organized. When students start answering correctly, unlock the next challenge by toggling the second challenge from "Hidden" to "Active."

LEVEL UP: For a truly immersive experience, download the "Drawing Pixel" lens from Snapchat and record yourself using the lens in front of a green screen. Find a Minecraft background to place yourself in front of, using a green screen app such as Do Ink's Green Screen!

CHECK OUR TUTORIAL VIDEO TO GET STARTED!

CLASS OR SCHOOL ANNOUNCEMENTS

PREP TIME:

LESSON FORMAT: Teacher and Student created

ACTIVITY DESCRIPTION: Record your school announcements using the Flipgrid Camera! Create a Group on Flipgrid where you can add daily announcements, then share the link or embed the video into a website of your choice!

FEATURES USED: Flipgrid Camera

TIPS AND TRICKS: Try using the TV screen .png image or the Breaking News Frame to fancy up your video!

AREA/PERIMETER EXPLANATION

PREP TIME:

LESSON FORMAT: Student created

ACTIVITY DESCRIPTION: Using the blocks filter, have students hold an object or colored piece of paper up so it can be seen on the screen. Using the draw tool, students can illustrate the area and perimeter of the object they are holding up.

FEATURES USED: Draw tool, Filters

TIPS AND TRICKS: Try having students submit videos without a final answer given. They can choose the objects and then draw on them, but they then submit the video for classmates to give answers to.

STOP MOTION

PREP TIME:

LESSON FORMAT: Student created

ACTIVITY DESCRIPTION: Create a stop motion video right within Flipgrid! Once you click on the record button, press the spacebar to quickly stop and start the video. Make any necessary adjustments to your video in between the pauses, but remember to keep them minimal so the animation appears fluent!

FEATURES USED: Flipgrid Camera

LEVEL UP: Try using the Flipgrid Stickers in your stop motion video! Create models that show the seasons, the rotation of the earth or the sun, or how plants grow.

CHECK OUR TUTORIAL
VIDEO TO GET STARTED!

AUGMENTED REALITY QR CODE CUTOUTS

PREP TIME:

SHARING SOCIAL

LESSON FORMAT: Teacher created

ACTIVITY DESCRIPTION: This is a great activity to display on a bulletin board or on "Meet the Teacher" night. Start by taking pictures of your students holding a white sheet of paper. Next, find a student's Flipgrid video QR Code. Download and cut out the QR Code, then glue it onto the picture of the student (place it over the white sheet of paper). Then, display so when scanned with the Flipgrid QR Code reader, they'll open up the response videos in Augmented Reality!

FEATURES USED: Flipgrid Camera, Flipgrid AR or QR Code Reader

GET STARTED HERE!

TIPS AND TRICKS: If using this technique on a bulletin board, try creating student portfolios in Flipgrid. By giving each student their own Flipgrid Topic, they can continue to add content, but you won't have to keep updating the bulletin board!

KIND MESSAGES

PREP TIME:

REFLECTION SOCIAL SHARING

LESSON FORMAT: Student created

ACTIVITY DESCRIPTION: This is a simple way to include SEL (social and emotional learning) into your classroom. Provide a space where your students can leave messages for one another. Encourage them to respond to one another's videos, and by doing so they will build the classroom community.

FEATURES USED: Flipgrid Camera

TIPS AND TRICKS: If you're worried about privacy, keep the Topic moderated. This will allow you to view the content before it gets shared with the rest of the class.

QR CODE IN A BOOK

PREP TIME:

DISCUSSION   REFLECTION   SHARING   GAMIFY

LESSON FORMAT: Teacher created

ACTIVITY DESCRIPTION: Create a video using the Flipgrid Camera, then download and print the video's QR code. Hide the QR codes throughout a book. We recommend using Scotch's Wall Tape to tape the QR codes into the book(s), which won't rip the pages when you go to take them out. Then, when your students find the QR codes as they read, they can scan them and be challenged with a task!

FEATURES USED: Flipgrid Camera, Flipgrid QR Codes

TIPS AND TRICKS: This activity can be done using a Group or individual Flipgrid Topic. If you create a separate Group on Flipgrid, you can then add Topics as you see fit. Looking for a simpler task for your students? Create a Flipgrid Topic, and then create your challenges under one Topic, where you would then post as a student, with students responding as replies.

GET STARTED HERE!

FLIPGRID AR TRADING CARDS

PREP TIME:

DISCUSSION   CREATION   GAMIFY

LESSON FORMAT: Teacher and Student created

ACTIVITY DESCRIPTION: Have your students use the trading card template below. Once they have finished the first card, have them record a response on Flipgrid. When the first video is done, download and print the Flipgrid QR code from the Educator's Dashboard. Resize and print (you can use something like Microsoft's PowerPoint to edit the QR Code sizes), then have the student cut out the QR code and glue it to the back of the trading card. Repeat this process for the rest of the cards!

FEATURES USED: Flipgrid Camera, Flipgrid AR QR Code Scanner

TIPS AND TRICKS: When your students record their videos, have them respond directly to themselves rather than adding a new reply each time. This keeps the Flipgrid Topic organized and easier to manage.

GET STARTED HERE!

IN OR OUT

PREP TIME:

DISCUSSION   REFLECTION   GAMIFY   SHARING

LESSON FORMAT: Teacher created

ACTIVITY DESCRIPTION: Using the features found in the Flipgrid Camera, create a four-box grid. In each box, place a different image. When providing your instructions, explain to the students that they are to think about which image out of the four should "go," or be removed.

FEATURES USED: Flipgrid Camera, Stickers

LEVEL UP: Try to create a situation in which there is not an incorrect answer, which will generate higher-level thinking skills and promote a greater class discussion.

WONDER BOARD

PREP TIME:

DISCUSSION   REFLECTION   SHARING

LESSON FORMAT: Student created

ACTIVITY DESCRIPTION: Integrate Flipgrid into your Genius Hour, 20% Time, or Wonder Hour by creating a Topic where students can share what they are interested in learning more about. Students can use various platform features to label their video so other classmates know what the topic of the video is. The teacher can then reply and attach links to the reply with a resource that the student(s) can use to get started with their inquiry.

FEATURES USED: Flipgrid Camera

LEVEL UP: Encourage your students to listen to the wonders and ideas of others and to join together with research and interests.

VIRTUAL WORD WALL

PREP TIME:

COLLABORATION REFLECTION CREATION DEMONSTRATE APP SMASHING

LESSON FORMAT: Teacher created

ACTIVITY DESCRIPTION: Use the Text feature inside the Flipgrid Camera to type words that you would like to appear on your virtual word wall. Record yourself reading each word, and then share the topic link with your students for easy access.

FEATURES USED: Flipgrid Camera, Text, Board, Draw

TIPS AND TRICKS: Use the Board feature to fill the screen, then add your text on top of the board. When you record yourself reading through the words, mark them with a circle or a dot so that you students can easily identify which word is which.

RECONSTRUCT A STORY

PREP TIME:

CREATION DISCUSSION REFLECTION DEMONSTRATE

LESSON FORMAT: Student created

ACTIVITY DESCRIPTION: Your students can easily retell what happens in a story by using the built-in Flipgrid tools. Have them use the board feature to create a background, stickers to represent characters, and even add a drawing to generate a personal flair.

FEATURES USED: Flipgrid Camera, Drawing

TIPS AND TRICKS: Tie this into the book "Stellaluna!" Students may add emoji stickers such as an owl, bat, moon, trees, and even take advantage of the "Galaxy" board (which you can find by clicking effects > board).

CHECK OUT OUR TWEET!

CHANGING THE SETTING IN FLIPGRID

PREP TIME:

REFLECTION DISCUSSION CREATION SHARING

LESSON FORMAT: Student created

ACTIVITY DESCRIPTION: Provide multiple creative outlets with this highly engaging activity! Allow students to change the setting of a text by drawing what they would change on a piece of paper. Then, on Flipgrid, have them explain what they would change and why they would change it!

FEATURES USED: Flipgrid Camera

LEVEL UP: For students who are reluctant to share their artwork, allow them to use the Flipgrid Draw and Emoji features to create a digital illustration.

CHECK OUT OUR TWEET!

LIVE WITH YOUTUBE

PREP TIME:

LESSON FORMAT: Teacher created

DISCUSSION SHARING DEMONSTRATE APP SMASHING

**CHECK OUR TUTORIAL
VIDEO TO GET STARTED!**

ACTIVITY DESCRIPTION: You can embed a "live" YouTube video into a Flipgrid Topic's Focus, which will allow you to be present with students in real time while they post on Flipgrid. Set up a live YouTube video, then copy the share link. Paste this link into the Flipgrid Topic Focus of your choice. When your YouTube video goes "live," your students will be able to see you in real time!

FEATURES USED: Flipgrid Camera

TIPS AND TRICKS: If students submit a Flipgrid response while you are "live," they will need to refresh the page to update the stream.

TRACING CHARACTER EMOTIONS WITH EMOJIS

PREP TIME:

LESSON FORMAT: Student created

REFLECTION DISCUSSION DEMONSTRATE

ACTIVITY DESCRIPTION: Dive deeper into a text by tracing the character emotions using the emojis in Flipgrid! After reading, allow your students to brainstorm what types of emotions the assigned character displayed throughout the text (for example: beginning, middle, and end). Have them explain their thinking by using the Flipgrid Camera and emojis that fit the character's emotions. Students also can respond to fellow classmates to discuss whether they agree or disagree.

FEATURES USED: Flipgrid Camera, Emojis

TIPS AND TRICKS: When we did this activity with our class, we let the students pause at various points in the text to think about how the character(s) were feeling. They then drew a picture of an emoji in a flow map to help sequence the emotions.

CHECK OUT OUR TWEET!

STUDENT PORTFOLIOS

PREP TIME:

LESSON FORMAT: Teacher and Student created

REFLECTION DISCUSSION
CREATION DEMONSTRATE SHARING

ACTIVITY DESCRIPTION: Create a Group for your class, then create a Topic for each student, using their name. When your students have class artifacts that they would like to preserve or share, have them explain it in a video in their Topic. At the end of the year, there will be a curated list of student work! Think of it like a digital portfolio, Flipgrid style!

FEATURES USED: Flipgrid Camera

TIPS AND TRICKS: Invite the families of your students by toggling on the "Guest Password," providing them with a window into the classroom that they can use over and over again throughout the year!

GET STARTED HERE!

FLIPGRID YEARBOOK

PREP TIME:

COLLABORATION REFLECTION SOCIAL SHARING

LESSON FORMAT: Teacher created

ACTIVITY DESCRIPTION: Create a Topic where your class can record videos of themselves for a Yearbook! Students can discuss their favorite things about their grade level, specific projects, or favorite learning moments.

FEATURES USED: Flipgrid Camera

TIPS AND TRICKS: If you're attempting to do this schoolwide, share your Topic(s) and then curate all of the submissions into one Group. Share the group as the "Yearbook!"

LEVEL UP: Take it to the next level by creating a Mixtape of your favorite video memories to create an epic end-of-the-year video for students to keep!

GRAB THIS READY–TO–USE LESSON DIRECTLY FROM THE FLIPGRID DISCOVERY LIBRARY!

CHARACTER COMPARISONS

PREP TIME:

CREATION DISCUSSION REFLECTION SHARING DEMONSTRATE

LESSON FORMAT: Student created

ACTIVITY DESCRIPTION: Have students of any age compare characters in a story, important players in history, and much more. Use text, drawing, emojis, and more to create visuals that students can voice over as they explain the similarities and differences between the two people.

FEATURES USED: Flipgrid Camera, Emojis, Text, Drawing

TIPS AND TRICKS: When working with younger students, try searching for relatable emojis ahead of time and giving students a list of what to look for to save time!

GET STARTED HERE!

Updates 3

Flipgrid truly cares about educators and takes their opinions seriously. Team Flipgrid is continuously updating the platform to meet the needs of educators and students globally. Learn about all the new changes and updates on our website:

SCAN HERE OR VISIT:

themerrillsedu.com/flipgrid/flipgridupdates

BIBLIOGRAPHY

Bland, Nick. *The Fabulous Friend Machine*. Markham, ON, Canada:
     Scholastic Canada Ltd., 2017.

Buzzeo, Toni, and Sachiko Yoshikawa. *But I Read It on the Internet!*
     Madison, WI: Upstart Books, 2013.

Collins, Suzanne. *When Charlie McButton Lost Power*. Logan, IA:
     Perfection Learning, 2010.

Cook, Julia, and Anita DuFalla. *The Technology Tail: A Digital Footprint
     Story*. Boys Town, NE: Boys Town Press, 2017.

Cook, Julia. *But It's Just a Game*. Chattanooga, TN: National Center for
     Youth Issues, 2013.

Daywalt, Drew. *The Legend of Rock Paper Scissors*. New York:
     HarperCollins, 2020.

Droyd, Ann, and David Milgrim. *If You Give a Mouse an IPhone: A
     Cautionary Tail*. New York: Blue Rider Press, a Member of Penguin
     Group (USA), 2014.

Menchin, Scott. *Goodnight Selfie*. Somerville, MA: Candlewick
     Press, 2015.

Polacco, Patricia. *Bully*. New York: G.P. Putnam's Sons Books for Young
     Readers; 2012.

Reynolds, Aaron, and Matt Davies. *Nerdy Birdy Tweets*. New York:
     Roaring Brook Press, 2017.

Willis, Jeanne, and Tony Ross. *Chicken Clicking*. London, United
     Kingdom: Andersen Press Ltd, 2015.

Willis, Jeanne, and Tony Ross. *Troll Stinks*. New York: Andersen Press
     USA, 2017.

ABOUT THE ILLUSTRATOR

MANUEL HERRERA is an educator, a speaker, and an illustrator. He specializes in sketchnoting, visual thinking, design thinking, and 3D printing and design. Over the past eighteen years, he has keynoted and led workshops at educational conferences, including SXSWEdu, ISTE, TCEA, MassCUE, FETC, and EDU. Manuel has illustrated books, publications, and graphics for a variety of organizations and schools. Currently, he is the innovation coordinator for the Affton School District and an adjunct professor for Webster University, both located in St. Louis, Missouri. In 2018, Manuel became a Google Innovator at LAX18, and in 2016 he was named the Midwest Education Technology Conference Spotlight Educator. You can follow Manuel on Twitter and Instagram at @manuelherrera33.

ABOUT THE AUTHORS

In addition to teaching, **JOE** and **KRISTIN MERRILL** share a love for vinyl records, college football, cold weather, and unplugged family time. They live in Naples, Florida, and when they aren't teaching, they enjoy spending time with their two sons Bryson and Baxson. They also enjoy traveling the world and meeting educators as they share their ideas and experiences through conference presentations and professional workshops.